# BEYOND DEATH

*"Christopher Scott is a true visionary of the Spirit—blazing trails for others to follow."*

—Peter Love, Ph.D., Founder of
The Center for Psychic Research Studies

*"Christopher Scott's Hyperdimensional Pure Energy Hypothesis will prove to be one of the most significant concepts of twenty-first century physics."*

—Patrick O'Brien, Mission Specialist,
NASA, JPL—Voyager, Galileo Projects

*"Christopher Scott's* ***Beyond Death*** *shines unprecedented new light on the most critical questions about physical and spiritual existence, and offers compelling evidence of life after death."*

—Richard Schroeder, M.D.

# BEYOND DEATH

## *Confronting the Ultimate Mystery*

Christopher Scott

Blue Dolphin Publishing

Published by Blue Dolphin Publishing, Inc.
P.O. Box 8, Nevada City, CA 95959
Orders: 1-800-643-0765
Web: www.bluedolphinpublishing.com

ISBN: 1-57733-077-3

Library of Congress Cataloging-in-Publication Data

Scott, Christopher, 1946–
Beyond death : confronting the ultimate mystery / Christopher Scott.
p. cm.
Included bibliographical references (p. ) and index.
ISBN 1-57733-077-3
1. Spiritualism. I. Title.

BF1261 .S45 2000
133.9—dc21

00-040322

Cover illustration by Gustave Doré
from Dante's *Divine Comedy.*
Cover enhancements by Jeff Case.

Printed in the United States of America

10 9 8 7 6 5 4 3 2 1

# PERMISSIONS

Bantam Books, a division of Random House, Inc. Carol Christiansen, Permissions Dept., for Stephen Hawking's quote from *A Brief History of Time.*

Burnham/Nelson-Hall Publishers, Richard Meade, Chicago, Illinois, for Harold A. Widdison's quote, and Dr. Raymond A. Moody's quote in *A Collection of Near-Death Research Readings* by Craig L. Lundahl.

Cordon Art, Margareth Verbakel, Baarn, The Netherlands, for *Other World, Still Life with Mirror*, and *Doric Columns* by M.C. Escher.

Ferguson Publishing Company, Andrew Morkes, Managing Editor, Chicago, Illinois, for quotes from *Man and His Symbols* by Carl G. Jung.

Harper Collins Publishers, for Marianne Williamson's quote from *A Return to Love,* and Dr. Dean Radin's quote from *The Conscious Universe.*

History Museums of San Jose, Paula Jabloner, Archivist, San Jose, California, for photographs of William and Sarah Winchester.

Pantheon Books, a division of Random House, Inc., New York, NY, third printing, 1961, 1962, 1963, Patricia Flyn, Permissions Department, for quotes from *Memories, Dreams, Reflections* by Carl G. Jung.

Princeton University Press, Loan Osborne, Permissions Coordinator, Princeton, New Jersey, for quotes from *Psychology and The Occult* by Carl G. Jung.

Swedenborg Foundation Publishers, Mary Lou Bertucci, Senior Editor, West Chester, Pennsylvania, for quotes from *A Compendium of the Theological and Spiritual Writings of Emanuel Swedenborg* by Emanuel Swedenborg, compiled and edited by Samuel S. Warren.

The British Museum, London, for the photographic image of the *a'shen* from *The Ancient Egptian Book of the Dead.*

The Winchester Mystery House, Shozo Kagoshima, Director of Marketing, San Jose, California, for all of the photographs of the Winchester Mystery House.

University of Texas Press, *The Ancient Egyptian Book of the Dead* translated by R.O. Faulkner, edited by Carol Andrews, Copyright © 1972, Revised edition 1985. By permission of the University of Texas Press.

Villard Books, a division of Random House, Inc. for Dannion Brinkley's quote from *Saved by the Light.*

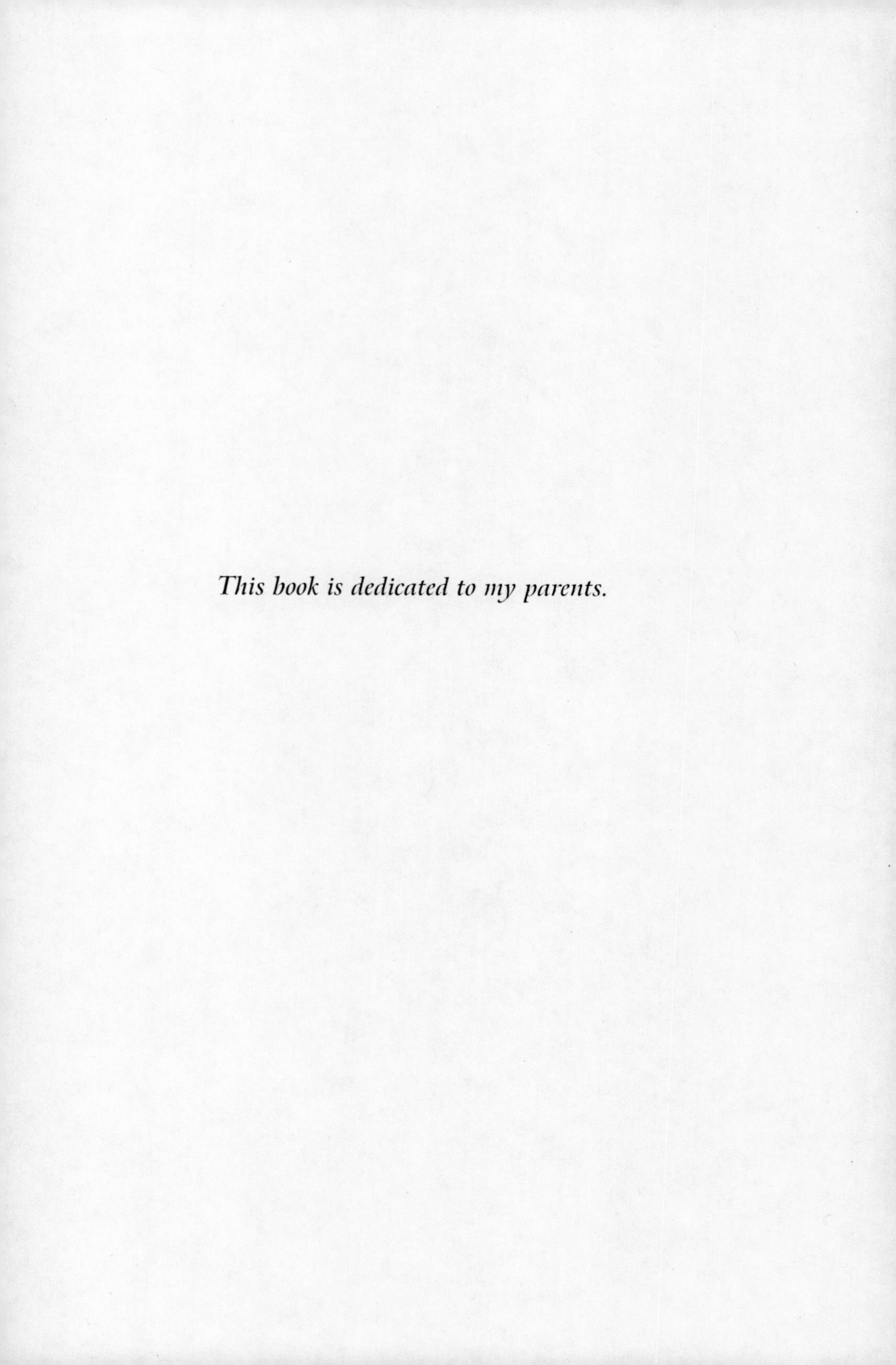

*This book is dedicated to my parents.*

# CONTENTS

# PREFACE

SO HERE WE ARE ... at the dawn of the third millennium, the age of Aquarius. We have come a long way—over the eons—we humans.

But who are we? What are we? Where are we heading? Does anyone know? Does anyone really care?

The other day I heard a man say, "nothing matters, we all just turn back into dust anyway." It was as if he was trying to say that, prior to our earthly existence, we were all equivalent to lifeless, non-entities. But if that were so, then, truly, where did the life-force within us come from? We would certainly ask the same question of an inanimate stereo or blow dryer magically coming to life without being connected to its Source.

Did we come all this way to simply resign ourselves back to the stars from whence the dust in our bodies derived? Is that all there is to it?

So much was missing from the man's vacuous statement—but, alas, I sensed its menacing sting. The past few centuries have taken their toll on the human race. Our quest for truth through scientific inquiry came at a gruesome price—we have sacrificed ourselves at the materialistic altar.

Back to dust? How pathetic! No ... we aren't here for that. Somehow we just got lost. And, somehow we need to find our way home. But to do that, we must go back to the Source—back before there was an earthly existence, back before there were even stars.

If we can go back to the Source, what will we find? Nothing? Everything? We will certainly find truth. But, contrary to the beliefs of scientific faith, truth will never be some object that can be observed or measured—Newtonian Physics and Quantum Mechanics are withering testaments to that.

Indeed, the laws of Newton, and Quantum Theory, flawed and incomplete as they are, would dissolve into oblivion upon coming face to face with the Source—and *that* would be an observable event because, once subjected to such a condition, space, time, and matter would cease to exist.

With an SSC, or "Superconducting Super Collider" (if we can ever get one), we would be able to make observations and calculations about the origins of our universe within the tiniest fraction of time permitted before confronting the Source: we might, for example, gain a glimpse of the apparent dichotomy between the "Higgs Phenomenon" and the "Conservation of Energy and Mass." That would be worth the price of a front-row seat. Or, possibly, the vast workings of the E(8) x E(8) symmetry arising from String Theory.

However, we will never see any of these dynamics, because they are all scientific phenomena, which, oddly enough, have never, and will never be observed—just taken on faith. And why should such intangible things merit greater faith over such long-abiding phenomena as angels (which have been observed over the millennia)? Go figure!

This brings us to the "Scott Hypothesis" which states that "ultimately, science must, one day, come face to face with what it cannot perceive or measure—and consider the mystical experience as being equal to an observation.

"If, on that day, we can re-create the energy of the Big Bang (probably with a Superconducting Super Collider), and take it back to the condition of the original 'Big Bang Singularity,' we will have to reach a critical point where all the material characteristics of 'the energy' will necessarily cancel themselves out—because, at that point, the laws which govern the material universe will break down—and matter, in any form, will not exist—neither will space nor time—and, hence, there will be nothing to observe.

"However, 'the energy' (the Source) will still remain (after all, energy cannot spring from nothing)—and that is *pure energy*, the energy we call *spirit*. Then, and only then will science achieve a glimpse of the mind of God."

Los Angeles
March 2000

# ACKNOWLEDGMENTS

MANY THANKS AND MUCH LOVE to all of those who have, directly or indirectly, been a source of wisdom, support, and inspiration throughout the writing of this book.

To my angel guides—my spiritual mentors (who tend to shun all manner of accolade), you have my deepest affection—always. To my other otherworldly mentors who have helped me to better understand the true nature of higher dimensions, most notably, St. Thomas Aquinas, Albert Einstein, M.C. Escher, Carl Jung, and Sarah Winchester—thank you.

And special thanks to all of the following: Shozo Kagoshima and the staff of The Winchester Mystery House, in San Jose California, for all your help, Margareth Verbakel and the Cordon Art, in The Netherlands, Sasha Coates of The British Museum in London, Mary Lou Bertucci and the Swedenborg Foundation, and, of course, my publisher, Paul Clemens, for his vision.

# INTRODUCTION

AT THE AGE OF SEVENTEEN I had the good fortune of studying under the tutelage of the Japanese Zen master, Henayana Roshi, at Claremont Men's College in Southern California. In accordance with Zen tradition, the classes were strict. Students would sit in a "lotus position," on a hard floor, staring at a fixed-point in space for hours on end. The purpose of this exercise is to become totally focused on the point of space that the observer is staring at—to such an extent that the observer and the "observed" merge together as one, unified entity. Thus, the observer is no longer the observer, and the observed is no longer the observed. Upon achieving such a transcendental state of consciousness, one is said to have attained a true look at reality. Such is the nature of INSIGHT.

At regular intervals during the "meditation period," a small bell would be rung, whereupon a student would arise from his or her lotus position and walk into an adjoining room to sit with the Roshi. The Roshi would look the student directly in the eye as if he was looking for a special gleam, a precious spark that he could instantly recognize as a glimmer of truth—not because the student was trying to deceive him, but rather because he was looking for a confirmation that the student had or had not "achieved" the consciousness of truth.

Typically, the Roshi would hold a long, narrow, bamboo stick in his hand. Should a student forget the purpose of the "sitting" and attempt to engage the Zen master in some vain, intellectual banter, a whack on the knee from the Roshi's stick would quickly remedy the matter.

Sometimes the Roshi would ask simple questions of the novice, like "How are you today?" Or "Are you enjoying yourself?" Or "Have you learned anything?" Actually, he wasn't particularly interested in conversing in the language of words. Rather he was looking for a response in the language of the soul—the language of intuition. A silent but knowing nod, or a certain, spontaneous smile would speak volumes to him.

On one occasion, as I sat with the Roshi, he pointed to a large bowl filled with water. "Put your hand in the bowl, grab hold of all the water you can, and pull the water out of the bowl," he instructed. My hand coalesced with the water, and as it swirled around, the water swirled with me, flowing with my every movement. I could see that my hand and the water were unified in a harmonious dance. Then I clenched my fist, trying to grasp as much water as I could—but the attempt was futile. The more I tried to hold on to the water, the more it eluded me. The water and I were no longer unified, we were separate, and THAT was a revelation. I had never before looked at the dynamics of trying to get a hold on water quite that way. Then, it hit me! An explosion of insight—trying to grasp water is like trying to grasp REALITY, like trying to grasp TRUTH!

The Roshi's eyes sparkled. He was reading me. I looked at him like never before—and, wearing a giant grin on my face, I proudly proclaimed, "Ah, now I get it!" WHACK! Actually, it was a delicate tap from the Roshi's stick. "No need to talk," he said. He was quite right. Trying to define the experience was like trying to grasp the water.

The Roshi's lesson produced an insight which showed me that no matter how hard we try to grasp reality, it has a way of eluding capture—staying beyond our reach. That is because reality is not A THING—it is an EXPERIENCE, therefore, it is not something to be KNOWN, rather it IS *REALIZATION.* Thus, the path to *realization* has never been a matter of acquiring knowledge. Knowledge, in the temporal sense, can be *invented.* But TRUE KNOWLEDGE cannot be invented. It simply IS—it always has been—it is the PROCESS of allowing an individual consciousness to merge with the greater, UNIVERSAL MIND. This is the path of INTUITION, the path by which INSIGHT comes to us like a brilliant burst of light.

This book is not about Death. It is about Life, and the reality of that life that is *Beyond Death.* Moreover, we cannot realize the truth of existence which transcends death without INTUITION and INSIGHT. Therefore, intuition and insight are central to the theme of this book—they are also central to the theme of *Spirituality,* regardless of the context with which one deals with or contemplates spiritual matters. Therefore, this book is also about the nature of *Spiritual Existence,* which, in temporal terms, invariably translates into manifestations of *Psychic Phenomena.*

Everyone experiences psychic phenomena, whether or not they care to admit it. Those who don't, tend to be in *denial,* dismissing their psychic experiences as delusion or fantasy—they fear they will be branded as being crazy or irrational. *Rationale* is a product of *material, spatial, temporal* existence. Within that context, rationale can serve as a useful tool—something we can grasp. But as we shall see in Part 2 of this book, space, time, and matter are entities which are designed to be grasped—to be defined. But trying to grasp reality (as we saw in the Roshi's lesson) only takes us further away from the true nature of reality.

This is also a book about confronting the duality that exists between science and spirituality. We cannot understand spiritual nature unless we understand what it is not. Therefore, a key element of this book involves an in-depth look at the nature of material existence. What is matter? What is it made of? How and why did it come into existence? And what role does the material universe play in our spiritual development?

Ultimately, we are all confronted with the question "What is death?" What do we gain by dying? And how do we truly know that life goes on after we die?

Finally, who or what is God? How does God fit into the universal equation? The answer is that God doesn't *fit* into the equation . . . God *is* the equation! But what does that statement mean to those who doubt God exists? All of us at one time or another have been confronted with questions of God's existence!

I once asked the Roshi if he believed in God. He told me to look into a mirror. "What do you see?" he quizzed. I responded, "I see myself." WHACK!

In some respects, this book is a gentle reminder of the Roshi's stick!

# PART ONE

# ANGELS: BEINGS OF LIGHT

# 1

# THE AWAKENING

***Happy those early days, when I***
***Shin'd in my angel infancy!***
***Before I understood this place***
***Appointed by my second race.***

Henry Vaughan

I AM FREQUENTLY ASKED how early in my life did I begin to notice the presence of angels, and when did I first become aware that they were communicating psychic insights to me. I can only say that, as far back as I can remember, angels have always been my constant companions.

As a child I merely assumed that everyone enjoyed the same special relationship with these magnificent beings of light that I had come to know. They would come to me in my dreams—always silent, warm, and assuring. They did not speak, but rather communicated with me telepathically in a symbolic-intuitive language that is perfect, clear, and precise. They would instantly whisk me off to a beautiful and different place. I used to call it, "The Place of Mirrors and Light"—it was my favorite place in the whole world (later in life I would come to realize that this was not a place at all, but, rather it is a dimension).

Every night I looked forward to my rendezvous with my angelic guides. There were always so many questions on my mind; however, I took great delight in the fact that the angels always knew what I was thinking, in fact, they always seemed to know my thoughts before I did. The beauty of this process was that, instead of teaching me through lessons and instruction, my angel guides incessantly filled my heart and mind with insight and inspiration.

By the time I had reached my sixth birthday, my intuitive exercises with my angel guides had become well developed. As a result, my insights became more heightened. I began to understand things about people in ways that defied any rational explanation. Sometimes this would get me into trouble. For example, my sister kept a daily diary which she always locked away in her desk drawer. Much to her chagrin, I would often recite to her, word for word, various passages, which she had secretly written in the little black book.

My mother knew about my special gift, and she wisely admonished me to be careful how I used it. How right she was! I had much to learn, and my journey into such matters had only just begun.

One fateful summer day, as I strolled to the neighborhood bus stop, I passed by an elderly gentleman sitting on a park bench. Suddenly I heard a voice in my head.

The voice called out my name: "Christopher!"

It was the kind of telepathic voice I was accustomed to hearing in The Place of Mirrors and Light.

Once again it called out, "Christopher!"

I turned to the elderly man seated on the bench. He had white, thinning hair and a rather seraphic complexion reminiscent of Santa Claus. Until that moment my encounters with angels had always been in the realm of The Place of Mirrors and Light.

I asked him who he was.

"You may call me Hobbs," was his reply.

I began fumbling for words, but he instantly read my thoughts.

"Ah, yes, you're wondering about my human appearance … blends in pretty good with the rest of the scenery, don't you think?"

As I stood in a dazed silence, Hobbs continued, "You're about to get on that bus over there to go to a swimming party."

"Yes," I replied. "I'm going to meet up with my friends."

Hobbs' gentle eyes grew somber. He said, "Christopher, if you choose to get on that bus, you will meet with disaster."

I looked over at the bus, attempting to ascertain the problem. When I looked back at the bench, Hobbs was nowhere to be seen … but I sensed he was not gone.

I took Hobbs' warning to heart. Without question, I knew, intuitively, that he was dead right. Later, that afternoon, I learned that the bus had been in a tragic accident. Hobbs, it turned out, was, and still is, my guardian angel.

The next few years of my life were complicated and confusing. In the innocence of my early years all that I had come to know of the world was the product of feeling. Attending public school was changing that. In the classroom the intuitions which I relied on and trusted were being invalidated by my teachers. Being "taught" to think seemed to me a natural contradiction of terms. This alien process of stripping feeling from thought was cloudy indeed.

Gradually, I felt myself slipping away from my angel guides, and they from me. Angels are attracted to quiet intuition and are repelled by noisy didacticism.

# 2

# THE REVELATION

***Sweet souls around us watch us still,***
***Press nearer to our side;***
***into our thoughts, into our prayers,***
***With gentle helpings glide.***

Harriet Beecher Stowe

JUST WEEKS BEFORE MY NINTH BIRTHDAY, I set out on my bicycle, riding the desolate, winding back roads that lay to the north of my home. As I approached a particularly treacherous bend in the road, my head suddenly became filled with a powerful voice, a voice I had heard before—it was Hobbs!

He said, "Christopher, be careful. If you don't slow down, you will be in danger!"

For some inexplicable reason I ignored Hobbs' warning. I "thought" I would be O.K., and then ... Bammm! I ran head on into a car traveling in the opposite lane. For a moment everything went black. There was a loud ringing in my ears.

Next, I realized that I was floating above the scene. As I looked down, I saw myself lying on the pavement. There were several people standing around my body. I heard one of them say, "I think he's dead." That statement surprised me because I wasn't in any pain.

Then, I felt like I was soaring higher and higher—everything turned black again. I felt myself flying into the blackness extremely fast. I wasn't frightened—in fact, I felt incredibly peaceful. I remember thinking, "I must be dead." Then, I saw a light. It was coming closer and closer, and brighter and brighter. I couldn't tell if I was moving towards it, or if it was moving towards me—it just kept getting brighter. It was a beautiful light, sort of clear white, like a brilliant jewel.

Somehow I was being drawn to the light through what seemed to be a vast tunnel. I felt like I was blending into the beautiful white light as if my essence, my very existence, was the light—it filled me with a love and understanding I had never known.

I was now more clearly awake and conscious than I had ever been. The light was now brighter than the sun, but it didn't heart my eyes—then I realized "these aren't my physical eyes, and this isn't my physical body," yet, somehow I still had a body. The light began to speak to me telepathically. It was the same kind of angelic communication I had always experienced in The Place of Mirrors and Light.

The light asked, "Is your life complete—are you ready to pass it over?"

Then the light surrounded me with a complete image of all of the events of my life up to that point. It was not like a movie. It was like reliving every moment of my life as a spectator, yet I could feel every emotion—not just my emotions—I could feel the emotions of everyone I had ever interacted with.

As I experienced certain events, I thought, "why did I do that?" or "I wish I could take it back or change it." While this was happening I thought, "this is weird, I'm experiencing my entire life in a split second—time doesn't really exist here."

Then I heard a powerful voice call me. It was unlike any angelic voice I had ever heard. It seemed to be coming from the other side of the universe, yet it was right there with me.

The voice said, "Understand!"

I was immediately filled with complete knowingness. In that moment I understood everything with total clarity, yet words cannot describe it.

Then the voice said, "You must decide if you are ready. Do you want to come with me or stay?"

I answered "stay."

I woke up in the hospital. There were doctors all around me, poking different parts of my body, asking if I could feel this or that. They seemed confused and stunned. Later, I was told that I had suffered a severe concussion, and it was a miracle that I was alive.

One doctor, Dr. Niemeyer, displayed a particularly keen interest in me. He kept asking me questions, especially about my "near death experience" (NDE). I sensed that behind his questions there was something even more profound gnawing away at him.

It was getting late. After much discussion Dr. Niemeyer finally went home. The events of the past few days had been extremely revealing, but when Dr. Niemeyer returned the next morning, IT HAPPENED—the greatest revelation of my life!

Dr. Niemeyer began with the usual chit-chat, but as he continued, I began to observe a purplish mist around his head. Then Hobbs appeared, standing to Dr. Niemeyer's left side. And then, just as suddenly, a boy spirit appeared, standing to the right side of the good doctor. Up to this point in my life, the only spirit beings I had ever seen were angels. The boy looked to be about my age.

Hobbs was direct and to the point: "Christopher, would you like to meet David?"

"Yes," I responded.

David and I began to engage in telepathic talk. Meanwhile, Dr. Niemeyer, who was oblivious to all that was going on, was also conversing with me. A strange sensation came over me as I realized that I was simultaneously communicating in two different dimensions. It was sort of like listening to a 45-rpm record and a 78-rpm record at the same time.

I stopped the doctor in mid-sentence. "Your son, David, wants you to know that the car accident was not your fault. He is happy where he is now, and he loves you very much."

Dr. Niemeyer's eyes widened, his mouth trembled. He asked, "Jeez, how did you know that?"

I replied, "David is here, and he is talking to me."

The doctor stood silent. He just looked at me with a slight smile and gave me a knowing nod, then left the room. From that moment on, I knew I was on this earth for a specific purpose.

In the years following my near-death experience, and the revelation about my ability as a medium, I discovered that there were many other people all over the world who had developed psychic abilities and had been through experiences strikingly similar to mine. I began reading every book about psychic phenomena I could get my hands on.

One book, in particular, caught my attention. It chronicled the life and work of a Swedish doctor and medium whose extraordinary life spanned the years of 1688 through 1772. His name was Emanuel Swedenborg. Throughout his entire life Swedenborg communicated with angels and spirits of the deceased. He even experienced near-death. I found his observations on spiritual communication to be quite remarkable. Swedenborg stated:

> **The speech of an angel or a spirit with a man is heard as sonorously as the speech of a man with a man; yet it is not heard by others who stand near, but by himself alone. ... The angels who speak with a man do not speak in their own language ... because angels, when they speak with a man, turn themselves to him, and conjoin themselves to him, and the conjunction of an angel with a man, causes each to be in a similar thought... Moreover, the thoughts of angels are not bounded and contracted by ideas from space and time, like human thoughts** (Swedenborg, 1854).

My ability as a medium was something I kept under wraps for many years—this was mostly due to the strange, disapproving looks I got whenever I tried to tell people

**Emanuel Swedenborg**

Courtesy of The Swedenborg Foundation

about my near-death experience—as a result, I learned to keep my mouth shut.

Shortly after I reached the age of seventeen, I discovered something new about myself. One evening, as I sat in my room, working on a school assignment, I reached across my desk for a pencil. The pencil was just barely beyond my fingertips. Suddenly, it rolled right into my hand. "How strange," I thought. Maybe it was an accident. I placed the pencil back where it had been, then held my hand just a few inches away from it. At first nothing happened. Then I tried focusing all of my thought on the pencil—only the pencil. Once again it rolled, obediently, back to my hand.

I began experimenting with other objects. Much to my delight, my newfound ability provided me endless hours of self-amusement. But I knew, intuitively, this was another gift from the divine source—like mediumship, it is not a toy. I went to the library and read about this psychic phenomenon called *psychokinesis* or *telekinesis*. It is actually an extension of our *auric field*. Some people have the ability to tune their auric fields towards the frequencies at which various physical objects have a natural resonance (more on this in later chapters).

Many people who have been through a near-death experience become sensitized to the higher frequencies of the spiritual plane, so it is not unusual that they display various psychic abilities—it may be manifested as *psychokenesis*, *psychometry*, *precognition*, *telepathy*, *mediumship*, or all of the above.

As always, my angel guides helped me to realize that my life would be meaningless if I allowed my special gift to be wasted. It is not wasted. It is my life's work.

I am often asked if I believe in God. My answer is how can I not? The voice that spoke to me during my near-death experience clearly came from God. I see all of the beautiful facets of God's creation at work every day. No matter what words people use to describe the God-force, they are talking about the same thing, just expressed in different ways. Mere words can never adequately describe who or what God is.

We are all participants in the God-force like drops of water in an infinite ocean. Angels are an integral part of the God process. They serve as our link to the higher power that dwells in us all. As finite beings, we cannot perceive or comprehend that higher power. Angels help us to understand the things that are a mystery to us. Like brilliant mirrors of light, angels reflect back to us the image of all that is divine.

# 3

# THE DYNAMICS OF ANGELS

***An angel stood and met my gaze,***
***Through the low doorway of my tent;***
***The tent is struck, the vision stays;***
***I only know she came and went.***

James Russell Lowell

WHAT ARE ANGELS? What is their nature? To begin, angels have awesome power. The Bible is full of passages in which angels say, "Don't be afraid." Their greatest power is that they know and understand all things.

St. Thomas Aquinas tells us that angels are intellectual, intuitive beings capable of instant, pure knowledge, the knowledge of truth, which he associates with the brilliance of light. Moreover, according to Aquinas, angelic light is an inner brightness that represents pure intelligence—this is what intuition is all about, and it is a vital function of angels to bring intuitive enlightenment to human beings. Aquinas states:

> **We humans have a dimness of intellectual light in our souls. But this light is at its full strength in an angel who ... is a pure and brilliant mirror** (Aquinas, 1947–48).

When I first encountered this phrase from Aquinas, I immediately reflected back to my childhood experiences of my angel guides taking me to what I then called "The Place of Mirrors and Light." It was there that I would nightly receive psychic insights about the temporal world. This was how I could wake up the next day and go tell my next door neighbor where he had lost his keys, or tell my father that the wheel bearing on our family car was about to disintegrate. I didn't need to question how I knew such things, I just knew.

The enlightenment that angels bestow upon us manifests in different ways. Usually it comes to us subtlety, quietly, and without fanfare. In fact, angelic enlightenment is usually preceded by what Aquinas refers to as the announcement of divine silence. He tells us:

> **Angels are announcers of divine silence. For it is clear that a conception of the heart or of the intellect that is without voice is with silence. But it is through a perceptible voice that silence of the heart is proclaimed... But it is necessary after something is announced to someone that they understand the announcement. In addition, therefore, because we can understand by the intellect the things that are**

> **announced to us through the angels, they themselves by the brightness of their own light help our intellect grasp the secrets of God** (Aquinas, 1947–48).

In other words, we cannot be open and receptive to angelic enlightenment if we are filled with noise and distraction. If we are not open, we can't receive. If we are not listening, we can't hear. This requisite is the underlying principle of all intuitive inspiration and insight. That is why meditation and prayer not only begin in silence, but are most effective when practiced in silence. This is equally true of the creative process. Creative people tend to find silence to be a perpetual source of inspiration.

Because silence is divine to angels, they are always drawn to it like magnets. Wherever there is silence, you can be sure that angels are present. Hence, the phrase "silence is golden." However, when Aquinas speaks of angels announcing silence, there seems to be a paradox in that statement, because announcing requires making sounds. No doubt this was an intentional device on his part in order to emphasize that angels do not communicate through a physical voice, but rather through telepathic intuition. In this way, angels speak to us through both our hearts and our minds—this is the psychic bond between them and us.

Sometimes "divine silence" is the key to removing barriers that stand in the way of my resolving important issues for my clients during private sessions. One case in particular comes to mind. The client's wife had recently committed suicide, and he was feeling a great deal of guilt because he had been unfaithful to her. Apparently, she had just learned of the affair before taking her life. He needed to know if she could forgive him.

During times of grief, guilt tends to act like a powerful radio frequency that drowns out all the other frequencies on the band. That was the problem. I was simply unable to pick up information from my angel guides because his intense guilt energy was, in essence, drowning out the signal. I had to teach him meditation exercises that would help him release the guilt.

Gradually the diffused, garbled energy became focused and still. The room instantly became filled with divine silence. There was a brief pause. Then, I saw the spirit of a young woman enter the room. She hovered for a moment over a lamp in the far corner, then stood directly behind him. I asked her if there was anything she would like to convey. She hesitated for a moment, then she began to communicate with me.

She told me that she had gotten extremely drunk before the suicide. She had been very distraught, and started taking sleeping pills, one after another. At some point, while swallowing the pills, she began to feel very sick. It was then that she had a change of heart and decided that she didn't want to go through with the suicide, but it was too late, she had taken too many pills.

She felt guilt about taking her own life. She said that her angel guides were helping her to overcome her guilt, and that she understood what her husband was going through. She then said, "tell Mark that I forgive him, and that I will always love him." With all of that said, she left. Needless to say, Mark was much relieved, and was ready to get on with his life.

Angels are strong-willed beings, and their will, above all, is to manifest love. Everything they do is motivated by love—that is because angels are devoid of vanity and self-love. However, their relationship with humans is not without conditions. Because they know our hearts and minds, angels choose when, where, how, and if they will become involved with us. If we want angels to come to us, we have to invite them in.

As is the case with divine silence, angels, because of their loving nature, are attracted to praise, particularly when it reveals itself in the triumph of the human spirit. For angels, this is the praise that mirrors the divinity that resides in us all—wherever there is praise, angels will be found. Conversely, angels shun arrogance, greed, and deceit.

The medieval theologian, Hildegard of Bingen, suggests that praise is the language of angels, and that praise (like silence) precedes understanding. Hildegard explained:

> **Just as sunshine shows the sun, so also angels announce God through their praise, and just as the sun cannot exist without its light, so also the Godhead is nothing without the angels' praise** (Hildegard, 1844-91).

As both Hildegard and Aquinas point out, there is a reciprocal interaction—a sort of give and take between angels and humans. Whenever humans solicit angelic intelligence, a hierarchical chain of events unfolds, all subject to our "free will." We have to earn our way to understanding the nature of divine mystery. It starts with the understanding that divine silence is a condition of purification, antecedent to enlightenment. If we choose to be enlightened, the angels literally empower us with the gift of insight (the first stage of psychic intuition).

Although, angels, by their nature, do not require gratitude, they do require humans to be responsible for their actions and to act positively, i.e., a positive attitude. Praise is the "divine attitude" through which we humans acknowledge the gift of insight.

Praise is the attitude of action seeking truth. Once we have satisfied all of these conditions, the angels may choose to bestow the gift of revelation upon us. This is powerful stuff, not to be taken lightly.

For humans, revelation is the highest expression of understanding. For angels, revelation is intervention.

The history of human development is one of angelic intervention spanning the scope of all cultures. Wherever and whenever sudden explosions of human ingenuity have arisen, such as tool making, the use of fire, the development of language, agriculture, mathematics, etc., all of the traditions handed down from generation to generation throughout the span of human existence, speak of receiving important knowledge and wisdom in the form of revelation coming from divine intervention from angelic beings. This can be seen in the cultures of the Aborigines of Australia, to the Native Americans, to the nomadic hunting and gathering societies that settled in the European, African, and Asian continents.

When I first saw the motion picture *2001: A Space Odyssey,* I was fascinated by Arthur C. Clarke's portrayal of early humans being given the gift of revelation through intervention from an advanced, extraterrestrial intelligence.

However, Clarke's cold, impersonal monoliths have no soul. They are a reflection of the Godless vacuum of a universe spawned by the Industrial Revolution of these past few centuries—an age which attempted to create a view of existence in its own mechanized image. This "Age of Enlightenment" (as eighteenth-century philosophers and scientists referred to it) was really an age of darkness. Angels were, for the most part, ignored or virtually forgotten, and the soul was swept under a dark carpet. Where there is darkness, there is a void of angels and psychic intuition. Ironically, the year 2001 promises to usher in a new age of renewed emphasis on spirituality and angelic revelation.

Angels also intervene in our lives as guardians. This too is a common theme in all cultures throughout history.

The ancient Egyptians called their guardian angels *a'shen.* As is the case with all guardian angels, one's *a'shen* served as both a guardian during his or her lifetime, and afterlife. Understandably, the *a'shen* was also symbolic of eternity.

For the ancient Summerians, Babylonians, and Assyrians, guardian angels served the dual purpose of protecting one's life and afterlife, and guardianship over one's crops. The carved stone reliefs of the Assyrians display an obsession with guardian angels, called the *Genii*, watching protectively over their fields.

The ancient Israelites not only had personal guardian angels, such as the three intervening angels who appeared to Abraham to warn him of Sodom and Gomorrah's impending doom, but they also had national guardian angels in the archangels Gabriel, Michael, and Raphael. Guardian angels are always with us. In my case, it's Hobbs.

a'shen from the *Egyptian Book of the Dead*

Life is all about making choices. When angels choose to become involved in our lives, they always allow us the free will of choice. Angels intervene, but they never interfere.

The alliance between humans and angels, as we've seen, is not passive; rather it is based on action, and action has to start with us.

Too many of us, on a day-to-day basis, choose arrogance over humility—we want to be right all the time. We become so wrapped up in our personal pride and ego that we can't "let go." It becomes a vicious cycle that engulfs us. We become our own prisoners, our own slaves. We allow ourselves to be swallowed up by the vain syndrome of not admitting when we are wrong, or that we are weak, or vulnerable, or, that we simply "don't know." This is our dark side, and angels choose to avoid it.

Pride is negative, praise is positive. Remember? It's an attitude. It is when we make the choice to acknowledge our shortcomings and our vulnerabilities, and call upon our higher power, that angels then rush in.

Hildegard elaborates:

> **If a human only sighs the name of its parent, God, then God calls the human back into proper behaviour and the protection of the angels rushes to the human's side so that they will no longer be harmed by their enemy** (Hildegard, 1844-91).

Once angels choose to intervene in our affairs, they never tell us what to do. That is not what divine intervention is about. They still offer us choices.

When Hobbs warned me about the danger of riding on the bus, he said, "if you choose to get on that bus, you will meet with disaster." Again, just before I slammed into the car, Hobbs warned, "if you do not slow down, you will be in danger." The choice was still mine. And when the voice spoke to me in the light at the end of the tunnel, it clearly gave me the choice of crossing over to the other side or going back to the physical realm.

Many of my clients have reported having similar experiences with their angel guides—they were all given the same power of choice.

Without a doubt, having free will is a key ingredient to being human. If there was no such thing as choice, we would never learn, and we are all here to learn.

# 4

# DO ANGELS HAVE WINGS?

***Around our pillows golden ladders rise,***
***And up and down the skies,***
***With winged sandals shod,***
***The angels come, and go, the Messengers of God!***

R.H. Stoddard

WE'VE ALL SEEN PICTURES AND STATUES OF ANGELS. We've even see angel jewelry. How is it that we have come to instantly recognize the depiction of an angel? Simple, they are always depicted as having wings. The idea of angels as winged beings has been with us since the beginning of time. However, the concept of angels in flight has more to do with the speed and freedom of movement associated with flight than it has to do with the actual act of flying.

Since angels are spiritual beings, and, therefore, have no physical bodies, it is impossible to know what they look like, because they don't really look like anything. It is useful for us humans to form a metaphorical image of angels in our minds, just as it was useful for Michelangelo to paint a metaphorical image of God on the ceiling of the Sistine Chapel.

During the thirteenth century, St. Thomas Aquinas wrote the *Summa Theologica*, in which he incessantly equates the nature of angels with the metaphor of light. However, upon closer examination, it becomes clear that Aquinas is not just speaking metaphorically. He is, in fact, describing the behavior of angels and light as if they are essential components of each other. For example:

> **An angel can Move in discontinuous time. He can be now here and now there with no time interval in between. When an angel moves, the beginning and the end of his movement do not take place in two instants between which there is any time... but the beginning is in one instant and the end in another. Between these there is no time at all. Let us say then that an angel's movement is in time, but not in the way that bodily movements are** (Aquinas, 1947–48).

In this one paragraph, Aquinas is describing the movement of angels much the way that a modern physicist would describe the movement of photons, particularly as it applies to Einstein's special theory of relativity. If we think of angels as photons, from the photon's perspective there is no passage of time occurring between the photon moving from one fixed point to another fixed point. Moreover, since photons (and angels) have no mass, nothing else in the universe can move faster "in the way that bodily movements are."

Aquinas also seems to be alluding to the fact that, for angels (just like photons), there is no difference between space and time. It is no wonder, then, that when Aquinas makes reference to angels as beings of light, he literally means it.

Aquinas' understanding of physics seems to be considerably more advanced than that of present-day physicists just entering the new millennium. Notice how Aquinas never asserts, or even implies that the movement of angels equates, in any way, with the speed of light (the ultimate speed in the universe). Speed has nothing to do with the instantaneous movement of angels. Furthermore, Aquinas clearly understood that angelic movement has nothing to do with traveling through space and time—it is interdimensional. Aquinas tells us:

> **An angel is in contact with a given place simply and solely through his power there. Hence, his movement from place to place can be nothing but a succession of distinct power contacts; and I say succession, because, as we have seen, an angel is not in more than one place at a time. And such contacts need not be continuous. ... The angelic movement too may be continuous. But it may, on the other hand, take place as an instantaneous transference of power from the whole of one place to the whole of another; and in this case the angel's movement will be discontinuous. ... We have already seen that the local movement of an angel can be continuous or discontinuous. When continuous it necessarily entails a passing through an intermediate place. ... This kind of movement—from one extreme of a given space to another, immediately—is possible for**

> **an angel, but not for a body; for a body is measured and contained by a place and so must obey the laws of place in its movements. Not so an angel: far from being subject to and contained by place. ... An angel can apply itself to a given place as it pleases, either passing through other places, or not** (Aquinas, 1947–48).

It is important to note that the nomenclature of the thirteenth century simply was not adequate to accurately convey Aquinas' thoughts. Notice that he avoids the word "travel." Aquinas also seems to struggle with the word "movement"—he constantly plants other phrases around it in order to better convey his meaning; e.g., "being in contact with a given place," and, "instantaneous transference of power from the whole of one place to the whole of another," and, "An angel can apply itself to a given place as it pleases, either passing through other places or not."

Aquinas also introduces two seemingly paradoxical terms: "discontinuous time," which really means an interval having no beginning or end, or passage of time, and "discontinuous movement," which really means an action in which there is no movement.

In other words, Aquinas is telling us that angels do not need to travel or move in order to instantly appear—even if it means instantly appearing on the other side of the universe. When angels appear somewhere, they just do it.

Hildegard's view of the metaphor of angels in flight perhaps offers the best summation of the subject:

> **Angels do not have wings as birds do, but fly many times as fast, at the same pace that human thoughts travel** (Hildegard, 1882).

I like this statement. It is consistent with my personal experience of angels—they dance around our thoughts. Their mobility and location, at any given moment, serves as a MIRROR OF OUR THOUGHTS.

# 5

# CAN ANGELS ASSUME HUMAN FORM?

***Angels and ministers of grace defend us!***

William Shakespeare

As I have stated earlier, angels, as spirit beings, do not have physical form. They don't need it. They can, however, show themselves to us as having physical form. In fact, they are master shape-shifters.

Although they have the capacity to manifest any likeness they choose, angels always appear to me in human form. They do this in two distinctly different ways. First, they may appear to us psychically by sending us a telepathic image (thought transfer). This is how Hobbs usually shows himself to me. I can see him, but the other people around me can't—this is also the way that spirits, other than angels, who have passed over to the other dimension, appear to me.

The second way angels show themselves to us is when they quite literally assume physical form and walk among us. This is typically the way guardian angels introduce themselves to the ones they have come to protect. It's the way Hobbs first came to me.

It still amazes me that people physically encounter angels every day without realizing it—the Bible makes note of that fact: "some people have entertained angels without knowing it" (Hebrews 13.3). It just goes to show, you never know who you are bumping into.

Whenever angels materialize, it is because there are situations which make it necessary to interact with us on our own turf ( the physical plane). Aquinas was well aware of this. He stated:

> **. . . angels are not themselves bodies, nor does their nature involve union with a body, we must conclude that they have sometimes assumed bodies. Hence angels do not need bodies for their sake but for ours** (Aquinas, 1947–48).

Guardian angels frequently intervene in our lives without our knowledge. There is an important reason for this. If they make themselves known to us, we may become too distracted to make correct choices.

Life choices can be like a complex road map. If we are in tune with our divine guidance, we will make correct choices. One correct choice leads to another, then another, then another, and so on. We have many life-paths to follow, all of them intricately connected to each other. Just one incorrect choice can create a domino effect which can turn one's life into an endless chain of disappointments and unfulfillment.

When guardian angels assume physical form and interact with us, it is for the purpose of assisting us in choosing a correct course of action—the following case study illustrates the point:

One of my clients, who is now the senior partner in one of the most prominent law firms in Los Angeles, told me of an angelic encounter which changed the course of his life. The encounter took place twenty-six years ago. My client had just passed the state bar exam. His former law professor had highly recommended him to a personal friend who happened to be, at that time, the senior partner of the same prestigious law firm.

It seems the firm had an urgent need to bring in a new junior partner. There were, of course, many experienced, highly qualified applicants to choose from. Because of the friendly recommendation from his former law professor, my client was granted a cursory interview with the head of the firm. The interview was scheduled for 9:30 A.M.

My client got up three hours early, impeccably grooming and dressing himself. He was in no hurry, and he drove carefully. Suddenly, his car's engine shut down. The car coasted to a dead stop right in the middle of the freeway. So, there he was, stuck in the frenetic, morning, rush-hour traffic. Still, there was no need to panic, he had plenty of time.

With cars whizzing past him, he bravely opened the hood of his car to fix the problem. But try as he did, his every effort failed to produce a remedy.

Time was now becoming the enemy. He began to get extremely frustrated. Nobody stopped to help. Gradually, as the minutes ticked by, his sense of helplessness turned into a sense of hopelessness. He began to entertain the idea of giving up—just leave the damn car in the middle of the freeway and make his way back home. It was too late to make it to the interview on time anyway.

He got back into his car and sat there for a moment, quietly thinking. Even though his situation was hopeless, he decided to try, one last time, to start the car's ignition. Of course, it didn't start. He began to laugh uncontrollably.

Suddenly, he heard the sound of someone knocking on the window. At first, he thought it must be the highway patrol. But no. Instead, it was an attractive, young woman. As he rolled down the window, she asked, "Do you need help?" "Yes," he replied. He asked her if she had jumper cables. Again, her answer was affirmative.

Before he knew it, their cars were side by side with cables in place. He tried the ignition. It still wouldn't start. Calmly, she asked him if he wanted her to push his car to the shoulder of the road. He responded, "Yes, please." What a relief!

He was amazed at her calmness; it was beginning to have a calming effect on him. Then he asked, "Would it be any trouble for you to give me a lift downtown?" Without hesitation, she agreed.

Before he knew it, they were parked in front of a row of tall buildings. He jumped out of the car, frantically searching for the address—it was right there in front of him, he was at the correct location. He turned around to thank her, but she was gone. He looked at his watch, it was 9:27 A.M.

As it turned out, the head of the law firm was so impressed with both my client's punctuality and his fresh, positive attitude that he hired him on the spot. He told me "it was as if a magical door had been opened for just a split second, and I could do no wrong."

As the passing years found him moving up the corporate ladder, he often reflected back to the mystery woman and the events of that fateful morning. He remembered every detail with total clarity, including the fact that he never told her the address. Deep down he knew that she had been sent to him to intervene in a pivotal moment of his life.

Two years ago, she appeared to him again. She looked exactly the same as she had looked twenty-four years earlier. This time, she revealed herself as his guardian angel. She warned him that if he chose to ride in the taxi he was about to enter, his life would be in imminent danger. Needless to say, he heeded her warning. The taxi, it turned out, had a fatal collision with a truck.

Whenever angels take physical form, and reveal themselves to us as our guardians, it is always for some urgent, life-altering, or, in many cases, a life-saving situation. The rest of the time, when they walk among us, they are like busy bees going about their work, blending into the crowd—much like the characters in the television series, *Touched by an Angel.*

In conclusion, Hildegard offers a perceptive description as to the way guardian angels blend in:

> **According to their nature angels are invisible, but they take their bodies from the atmosphere and appear visible in the human form to those they are sent to as messengers. They also adopt other human**

**habits. They do not speak to humans with angelic tongues, but instead with words that can be understood. They eat as humans do, but their food evaporates like dew ...** (Hildegard, 1844-91).

# PART TWO

# UNRAVELING THE MYSTERY

# 6

# THE HYPERDIMENSION
## *The Other Side of Existence*

***You can recognize truth by its beauty and simplicity... because the truth always turns out to be simpler than you thought.***

Richard Feynman

THREE CENTURIES AFTER AQUINAS, a revolution in scientific methodology and philosophical inquiry took place. The works of Copernicus and Galileo shook the very core of Western thinking—paving the way for the emergence of a new, mechanized view of the universe, spawned chiefly by Isaac Newton. Newton's *Principia Mathematica* laid the foundation for modern physics and a radical new way of looking at the nature of existence.

God and the angels were no longer regarded as essential in the universal equation. All things could now be empirically explained as being cogs in a vast cosmic machine.

Understanding the secrets of nature had become a simple matter of peeling back layer upon layer to reveal how each microcosmic mechanism in the macrocosmic "machine" worked.

By the end of the nineteenth century, scientists generally held the arrogant notion that they stood on the brink of unlocking the ultimate mysteries of the universe. After all, Newtonian physics, along with James Clerk Maxwell's field equations, had engendered a fertile comprehension of gravity, and electromagnetism—there were only a few layers left to peel before humanity would become the master of all creation—so it seemed.

The dynamics of the three spatial dimensions of height, width, and depth had a mathematical certainty about them that filled us with an intoxicating reverence for our ability to calculate, with near precision, the movements of all the stuff the universe is made of. Then too, our knowledge of how the stuff (matter) is constructed appeared to be a foregone conclusion.

But somehow, new pieces to the universal puzzle kept cropping up—if only we could find a little more space to work with, we could then finally wedge the elusive pieces permanently into place. New concepts of a possible fourth spatial dimension began to creep in. But could such a dimension actually exist? What kind of space would we find there? Did we really comprehend what space is?

The coming of the twentieth century saw a brief dalliance with fantasies of a fourth spatial dimension—it became a fashionable rage.

Various scientific societies, and a score of nefarious individuals, trying to pass themselves off as "authentic" psychics and mediums, entertained each other with endless hours of idle speculation and absurd attempts to demonstrate all the imaginable and magical vagaries a fourth dimension could possibly conjure about the still hidden mysteries of existence. However, the idea that other dimensions could exist had taken a revolutionary bite out of the absolute authority of Newtonian dogma—the refractory roots had been firmly planted. A new tide of innovation, the likes of which had never been seen, was about to unfold.

In 1905, a young clerk working in a Swiss patent office, by the name of Albert Einstein, came to the simple but stark realization that all things in the universe are ultimately measured by their relationship to the speed of light. In other words, if a physical object stands at rest or rockets off at an incredibly high velocity, the speed of light, in either instance, remains exactly the same, relative to the object's point of view—that is because *time* slows down or speeds up in direct proportion to how fast or slow the object is moving.

The *c velocity*, or speed of light, therefore, is the only *constant velocity* in the universe—moreover, it is also the supreme speed limit. It is physically impossible for anything else to move as fast or faster than light. But why? The answer is that all physical objects in our universe have *mass* or weight (unlike light, which has no mass). Furthermore, Einstein reasoned that mass and energy are two *equivalent* aspects of the same thing—the energy that is expended in an object's movement is converted into mass. Therefore, the closer an object comes to moving at the *c velocity*, the more it gains weight, or mass. Mass, therefore, acts as a kind of automatic breaking system. So, as the object races towards the *c velocity*, its fat mass increases to infinite proportions (larger than the universe itself). No matter how hard it tries, the object can never reach the *c velocity*.

Through this profound discovery Einstein deduced that time is, in fact, the fourth dimension—as a result, all of the energy and matter in space and time could now be seen as being unified—this principle, called *Special Relativity*, is expressed in Einstein's famous mathematical equation, $E = mc^2$ (*Energy equals Mass, times the speed of light squared*).

Einsteinian Relativity turned the scientific community completely on its head, changing history forever. Yet, it still didn't explain everything. There were still more unwieldy pieces of the puzzle popping up.

Despite the success of Special Relativity to unify energy and matter, the pursuit to understand the workings of existence remained as far beyond our reach as did the speed of light. Unifying matter and energy was one thing, but unifying the four natural forces, i.e., gravity, electromagnetism, the strong nuclear force, and the weak nuclear force was quite another thing. Somehow, it seemed, more space was needed.

In 1919, a German mathematician named Theodr Kaluza showed that light and gravity could be unified in a "higher" fifth dimension. Although the "Kaluza Klein Theory" still neglected to unify the four natural forces, it did point theoretical physics in the right direction; however, it would be another sixty years before the significance of higher dimensions would be realized by the scientific community.

As the world of theoretical physics plodded along during the early decades of the twentieth century, the art world was quick to jump onto the higher dimensional bandwagon. Cubist painters, such as Pablo Picasso and

Georges Braque, were churning out stunning images depicting a new perspective that went far beyond the archaic three dimensional view of reality.

The observer was now compelled to wonder, "What does the ultimate nature of reality look like? How are we to perceive it? Is there a higher perspective or medium through which we can perceive it?" In response to such questions, the Dutch artist, M.C. Escher, spent the better part of his life seeking higher truth in the order and unity he saw at play in higher dimensional geometry.

Escher's art revealed both his fascination and torment with the concept of infinity. Likewise, he was equally obsessed with expressing different ways to tear down the walls of three-dimensional space. But, unlike the Cubists, Escher wasn't content to just show the observer a simultaneous, three-dimensional view of something, which could only be seen from another dimension—such artistic representations of a higher perspective of reality (however brilliant) still conveyed only the quality of a multi-faceted facade.

One of the most prominent devices Escher used in his art to convey higher dimensional relationships was the mirror. He realized that mirrors reflect back an image representative of a fourth, spatial dimension. When we view ourselves in a mirror, we see ourselves simultaneously occupying two distinctly separate points in space. Of course, we see this image as an illusion. Nevertheless, it is an image which transcends the boundaries of space and time. Moreover, it shows us a true feature of how things look from a higher dimensional point of view.

Escher wanted his art to transcend what he regarded to be clever tricks—he wanted it to be truthful in the sense that it showed us higher dimensional perspectives that we could see to be logically and mathematically precise. Furthermore, Escher saw his art to be a reflection of a dimension of pure thought which exists as an eternal, immutable reality. Escher said:

> **the spherical world cannot exist without the emptiness around it, not only because "inside" presumes "outside" but also because in the "nothing" lie the strict, geometrically determined, immaterial middle points of arcs. ... There is something in such laws that takes the breath away. They are not discoveries or inventions of the human mind, but exist independently of us** (Escher, 1971).

It is interesting to note that Escher felt a greater kinship with mathematicians than he did with other artists.

The Kaluza Klein theory was a brilliant achievement. It not only unified light and gravity but succeeded in unifying the field equations of Einstein and Maxwell. In fact, light could now be explained as a vibration from the fifth dimension.

But the scientific community wasn't ready to deal with a fifth dimension for two fundamental reasons: first, there was tremendous skepticism that such a dimension could actually exist. Unlike the fourth dimension of time (which, by itself, was not regarded as being spatial), the fifth dimension being proposed by Kaluza Klein was spatial. Understandably, this presented problems. Physicists were forced to ask, "Where is this other space? Why can't we see it or detect it? The convenient answer that came back was, "It can't be detected because it is curled up in a tiny ball the

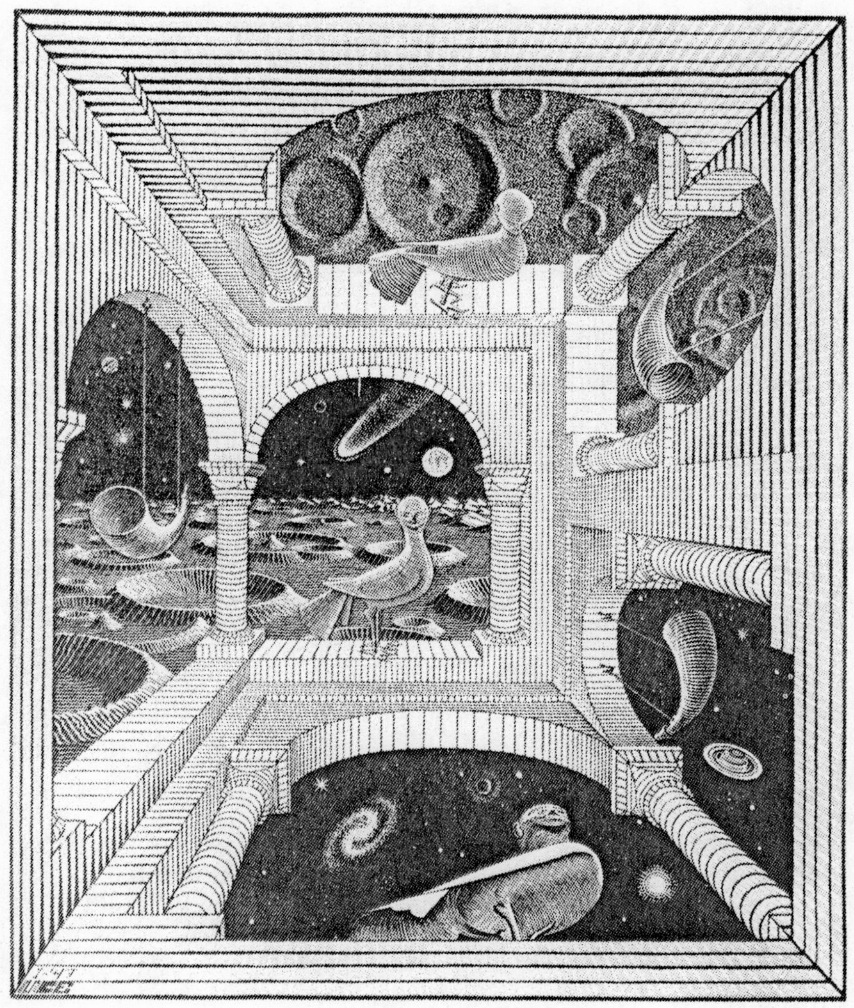

**Other World**
By M.C. Escher

size of a *Planck length*" (about 100 billion billion times less than a mere proton).

The second reason Kaluza Klein Theory got lost in the shuffle was due to the advent of an exciting, new theory called *quantum mechanics* (to be discussed later). Physicists would be immersed in "Quantum Theory" for the next six decades before they would have another serious look at the realm of higher dimensions.

The concept of higher dimensions, however, didn't vanish into thin air. Einstein, for example, entertained the idea, off and on, for the rest of his life—after all, it was he who started the whole thing.

Perhaps the most disturbing aspect of higher dimensional thinking, from the physical point of view, was that its advocates were always pushing for more space in order to create more beautiful mathematical equations in their ongoing quest for unification.

Through "Special Relativity," Einstein had brought unification to the duality of space and time—yet space and time are still uniquely different entities unto themselves.

Clearly, the dualistic boundaries separating space and time had not been overcome because more space had been added, but rather because more perspective had been introduced into the equation. This was accomplished by means of a mathematical tool (or trick) called a "metric tensor." Simply put, this means using a mesh of "imaginary numbers" or values through which we can visualize a simpler, more cohesive view of things from a higher, geometric perspective. To better understand how this works, let's use a simple analogy. Imagine you are constructing a building just like one of the towers of the New

York Trade Center. But instead of seventy stories, you keep adding more stories, thousands, perhaps millions of stories—we know that's not physically possible unless we use some kind of support structure that will prevent your seemingly impossible building from tumbling down. So, for the sake of argument, let's bring in some gigantic cranes that reach all the way to the top of your building to hold it securely in place. Now imagine the cranes are invisible—they're holding the building up, sure enough—we just can't see them. That's basically how metric tensors and "imaginary numbers" work in field equations.

The mathematics supporting the existence of higher dimensions is quite valid—in fact, the math truly compels us to acknowledge their existence. We are further compelled to acknowledge that *all things become simplified and unified in higher dimensions.*

But are higher dimensions really spatial? Special Relativity had found the fourth dimension to be temporal rather than spatial. Unquestionably, Kaluza had given us solid, mathematical proof of the existence of a higher, fifth dimension—but describing it as a curled up ball the size of a Planck length could hardly qualify it as a plausible dimension of space. No, higher dimensions must, in ways not yet clear to theoretical physics, transcend space and time.

The 1960s (among other things) saw a revived interest in higher dimensions due largely to the decline of enthusiasm for Quantum Mechanics, and the introduction of new mathematic, symmetrical models, most notably the *Ramanujan modular function* (see Glossary, page 210).

Through the long-lost equations of the East Indian mathematician, Srinivasa Ramanujan, theoretical physicists, who were still searching for "more space" to give them the ultimate unification theory, found, in Ramanujan's mathematics, not five, but ten dimensions. This became the critical ingredient in the genesis of a new hypothesis called "String Theory" (see Glossary, page 212). By the 1980s, it would be called "Superstring Theory."

So, what was the origin of the ten dimensions—where did they come from? We are all familiar with the event called The Big Bang, the initial act of "Creation" which led to the formation of our universe and everything in it that is made of matter ( i.e., things which have mass, or, weight). According to the current "Superstring Theory" the reality which preceded The Big Bang did not include matter. Because matter didn't exist, space and time didn't exist.

Space and time are not really things; rather they are more like mathematical expressions which describe the relationship of one material object to another. As we shall see, without the existence of matter, space and time have no meaning.

So, what did exist? From a physical perspective, theoretical physicists don't know. However, from a mathematical perspective they do know, with certainty, that some sort of entity existed as a ten-dimensional reality, infinitely curled up in a ball the size of (you guessed it) a Planck length—however, since space didn't yet exist, I think it would be more accurate to call it zero space.

Whatever this entity's nature was, remains a mystery. We do know, however, that its ten-dimensional state was not quiescent—it was active, and it either contained, or was contained by, an awesome primal energy.

At some point, four of the ten dimensions, in essence, rotated and fractured, or, put another way, flattened out, leaving the other six dimensions in their curled up state. This *flattened out condition*, in turn led to the cataclysmic explosion of The Big Bang which resulted in the expansion and development of the universe we now know.

But what of the other six dimensions? Are they really spatial dimensions, as String Theorists suggest, or are they something else? My purpose here is to provide the reader with a fundamental understanding of the origin of the physical world we live in, and the immaterial dimension which transcends it.

Just picture in your mind a balloon covered with a lot of black dots. As the balloon expands, it is like our universe after The Big Bang. As it continues to expand, the dots, representing galaxies and clumpy clusters of stars, move farther and farther away from each other. However, the source of the balloon's expansion cannot be located anywhere on or about the balloon's four dimensional plane (i.e., height, width, depth, and time)—its causation has to originate from some source other than itself.

In the case of our universe, the source of its origin, and subsequent expansion, is the same as the other six dimensions, which I shall refer to, collectively, as the *hyperdimension*.

Since the hyperdimension does not exist in space or time, it cannot be located in any place. Yet, it is right in front of us—it is all around us hiding in plain view.

Although the hyperdimension still shares the same original, pervasive relationship with the four dimensions of space-time, it shares none of its qualities or characteristics. Moreover, the hyperdimension *flows* through space-time, yet, space-time cannot flow through the hyperdimension. Furthermore, the hyperdimension is neither finite nor is it infinite—this is similar to Stephen Hawking's idea that the universe is finite but has no boundaries. The difference, here, is that Hawking's concept (in my view) describes the fuzzy, gray area where space-time ends and the hyperdimension *simply IS,* whereas the hyperdimension is immune to such space-time descriptions as *finite* and *infinite* because it transcends space-time.

The hyperdimension is not a place or a thing—it is more a process whose essence is *pure thought*—the essence of *spirit*.

St. Augustine said, "Whatever is not matter is spirit." Pure thought or spirit does not need to travel or move. It is all pervasive. It is the underlying attribute of divinity, and divinity is present everywhere, in everything.

In his novel and motion picture, *Contact,* Carl Sagan offered us a portrayal of interdimensional travel via a giant machine requiring an extremely high ratio of energy for its operation. That's nice for sci-fi, but it has nothing to do with accessing the hyperdimension. However, much to his credit, Sagan did understand that contact with higher dimensions ultimately is a function of *mind* that is beyond space and time.

The real process of making contact with the hyperdimension is through the activity of the *soul*—in other words, it is, by its nature, psychic. The word "psychic" is Greek, meaning "of the soul."

## What Is the Soul?

The concept of the soul has been around as long as there have been human beings. Since everyone has a soul, it would seem to be a simple matter to describe it, yet, I've found people have difficulty in doing just that. To me, this is understandable. After all, your soul is what your life is all about. It's who you really are. It is also the ineffable link to the great mystery of what lies beyond our temporal lives.

The dictionary defines the soul as:

> **the immaterial essence, animating principle, or actuating of an individual life: the spiritual principle embodied in human beings, all rational and spiritual beings: a person's total self: an active or essential part** (Webster, 2000).

Unquestionably, this traditional view of the soul conveys an apt description of its characteristics, yet it says nothing of its dynamics.

So, what is the dynamic essence of the soul? The answer is that it is a construct of pure energy—the unifying principle of life itself. But is it the same energy of the electromagnetic force, or the energy of the strong nuclear force, or the energy of the weak nuclear force? No, because these are the energies of the material dimension of space-time and are, therefore, subject to the laws governing space-time.

The pure energy of the soul is immortal—it can neither be destroyed nor can it ever die, because it doesn't exist in the limited structure of space-time. It exists in the *eternal now*.

There is, however, one aspect which the spiritual energy of the soul, and the energies of matter do share: *containment*. The energetic forces of matter are contained by what physicists refer to as invisible fields; e.g., the energy of the electromagnetic force is contained by the invisible electromagnetic field. The energy of the strong nuclear force is contained by the invisible gravitational field, etc.

Spiritual energy is contained much the same way that fields contain the energies of matter. But instead of a field, the entity containing our spiritual energy is the soul. In other words, the soul is not contained inside the body, rather the body is contained by the soul—but just like fields, souls do not have distinct boundaries. Moreover, just like a field, the soul is the synergistic whole that unifies the components of the spirit, i.e., pure energy, consciousness, and thought.

Furthermore, the activity of the soul is like the activity of waves and vibrations of fields. A soul's energy is active through vibration and resonance. This is the dynamic essence of what mystics and psychics refer to as the "astral body." It is that aspect of our soul which contains not only our thoughts, but also the psychic image of our physical body, much like a spiritual version of a photographic negative.

Whenever I communicate with spirits of the deceased, it is their astral body that I see in my mind's eye. Also, unlike dense matter, which vibrates at extremely low frequencies, the astral body resonates at extremely high frequencies.

When we dream, our astral body transfers from both our physical body and the physical plane of space-time into the spiritual realm of the hyperdimension. This is called "astral projection" (I will discuss this in more detail in Chapter 13).

When the transition we call death occurs, the astral body, along with the rest of the soul, takes permanent leave of the physical body, and resides in the mind of the hyperdimension. I know from personal experience that whenever these events take place, angel guides are always present.

## After-life

I think there are few words adequate enough to describe life's transition from the physical dimension to the spiritual dimension. The word "death," without a doubt, is the least adequate. Death literally means the end of life, period. The concept of death totally denies the existence of spirit, and assumes, somehow, that the life-force is a material object.

It is no wonder, then, that philosophers such as Plato and Hildegard use the word "dissolution," whenever they talk about the transitional phase of life. Dissolution means that the body simply dissolves, leaving the living soul intact to continue with the business of pursuing its purpose of existence—namely, the purpose of evolving spiritually.

Both Plato and Hildegard recognized that the transitional phase of life is a creative act. In other words, they understood that even after dissolution, life is still a learning process; we still have choices to make. They further emphasize the divine role that angels serve in guiding us as we continue to make choices which affect our spiritual development. Plato elaborates:

> **Now this way to the other world is not a single and straight path—if that were so, no guide would be needed, for no one could miss it; but there are many partings of the road** (Plato, 1942).

The motion picture *What Dreams May Come* touches on a number of critical after-life themes, particularly the film's emphasis on the notion that after-life is a process of evolving or devolving to either higher or lower levels of spiritual existence based on the choices we continue to make.

Moreover, the film stresses the need of guidance from more highly developed spirit beings. But most importantly, the film provides the insightful view of the spiritual domain as a dimension of mind. In this regard, the film renders the allusion that heaven or hell is a construct of our individual state of mind, which reflects the level of our spiritual growth.

Heaven or hell is not a physical place—it is a state of existence which we, ourselves, create, and it is up to each of us to decide which level of existence we choose to be at.

We are all individual aspects of a greater collective soul, a Divine Mind, the essence of which is pure thought and brightness. The choices each of us make, and the spiritual lessons we learn, determine how close or how far from the brightness we will be.

Clearly, the ultimate state of existence is not material in nature, rather it is spiritual. But what does that mean? What is the ultimate state of existence made of?

**Figure 1**

*Figure 1 shows two equilateral triangles made of six identical match sticks. This is a puzzle designed to demonstrate the simplifying nature of higher dimensions.*

*Problem: construct two more of these triangles for a total of four equilateral triangles of the same proportions using the same six match sticks.* *For the answer, see page 221.*

## 7

# EXISTENCE REALLY IS MIND OVER MATTER

***The stuff of the world is mind stuff ...***
***the mind stuff is not spread out over space and time!***

Arthur Eddington

***I want to know how God created this world.***
***I am not interested in this or that phenomenon.***
***I want to know his thoughts, the rest are details.***

Albert Einstein

TWENTY-FIVE CENTURIES AGO, an obscure Greek philosopher named Anaxagoras proposed that "Mind" is the origin and cause of everything. He further maintained that through a process or event which he referred to as "rotation," Mind became the initiator or prime mover which created all matter.

Moreover, the rotation which produced the material state of the universe that we now know, will, over an indefinite period of time, "accelerate" and "cover a still wider area" (in other words, it will expand).

However, at some point prior to the rotation, Mind existed as a "mixture." In this mixture, "all things were present, infinite in number, yet infinitesimal in size, not revealed because of their smallness" (or, in the parlance of modern physics, it existed in zero space).

The rotation of the mixture also resulted in "a separation" of the mixture's components. Additionally, following the separation, Mind and mixture were no longer the same thing, however, Mind is somehow "in contact with, if not present in all things." Moreover, "Mind has knowledge of everything, and controls all things that have life."

The doctrine of Anaxagoras was widely misunderstood and ignored by both his contemporaries and subsequent generations over the millennia. In fact, the mystique of his ideas remained obscure until the recent advent of "Superstring Theory" in theoretical physics.

Anaxagoras, on one hand, is giving us, I think, an uncanny description of the original ten-dimensional state of the universe, its separation of dimensions (i.e., six dimensions and four dimensions), resulting in the creation of matter (The Big Bang), and its subsequent expansion.

On the other hand, he wraps it all up in virtually the same *prime mover* doctrine later expounded by St. Thomas Aquinas. Also, it is important to examine Anaxagoras' uncanny use of the word "rotation." He uses the term *rotation* much the same way that modern physicists use it to describe the principle which underlies the dynamics of space-time.

When viewed from the perspective of higher dimensions, space and time are indistinguishable from one another because they *rotate* into each other. They are different sides of the same imaginary coin. If we give the coin one rotation, we have the dimension of time. If we give the coin another rotation, we have the dimensions of space and vice versa. This is why physicists have connected the words space and time together as one term, *space-time*.

There is, however, a third side to the coin: matter. After all, at the atomic level, matter is 99.9% empty space (or, what some physicists refer to as "imaginary space"). So, if we rotate the coin in another direction so that it lies flat, exposing its edge, we then have matter. Space, time, and matter are all different aspects of each other—any one aspect cannot exist without the other two.

But what is the meaning of matter, and what is it made of? The reason I pose this question is because we cannot fully understand the nature of *spirit* without a better understanding of the nature of *matter*.

Quantum physics has sought to explain the nature of matter by reducing it down to its most finite components, beginning with the basic particles of atomic structure, which are made of even smaller, composite, sub-atomic particles, which, in turn, are made of still smaller particles called "quarks," and so on. However, the word "particles" (quanta) must not be confused with what we conventionally perceive to be concrete, physical objects such as particles of dirt or sand, etc. Quantum particles are a seemingly endless chain of tinier units of energy.

In fact, the dictionary defines a particle as:

> **a minute quantity or fragment: a relatively small or the smallest discrete portion or amount of something** (Webster, 2000).

Without a doubt, the concept of point particles has proven to be useful as a technological tool, but quantum reductionism still does little to help us understand what matter is, because, invariably, we end up with an infinite number of boxes within boxes within boxes to the point of absurdity. Therefore, it is futile to think of matter as being made of smaller and smaller versions of itself, ad-infinitum. There has to be some other source and cause of its existence.

Einstein was a notorious critic of quantum mechanics. He saw that matter is not a thing, but rather is a *process*—a construct of energy bound within fields, or, put another way, matter is an illusion created by the resonant velocity of different kinds of energy. In other words, the structure of matter is ultimately derived from an *immaterial* source.

As we enter the twenty-first century, the idea of point particles as the ultimate building blocks of matter has been replaced by the idea of tiny vibrating strings.

According to the new String Theory, the structure of all matter is comprised of a complex number of differing waves or modes of resonance emanating from the strings. Theoretically, if the strings could be seen, we would (once again) find their diminutive size to be about the size of a "Planck length," i.e., about 100 billion billion times less than a proton.

The function of the strings is likened to the function of vibrating guitar strings or violin strings. When they stretch or contract, they vibrate at higher or lower frequencies. Thus, matter is literally made of a kind of harmonic music.

How do we know these strings exist? Actually, we don't. After all, strings cannot be empirically seen or detected. However, the math forces us to acknowledge that "something" exists as a "self-perpetuating" source of the "Super Resonance" from which all matter is made. In other words, strings, or something that behaves like strings, must exist much the same way we knew of the existence of the outer planets of our solar system long before we could see them. The mathematical proof serves as evidence that a source of the Super Resonance must exist—that, in itself, is not necessarily in dispute. What is in dispute is the nature and origin of "The Source." Is it simply a self-perpetuating (String Theorists prefer the words "self-consistent") mechanism, or is it something much deeper, still well beyond our comprehension?

Be that as it may, the advanced mathematical equations of Superstring Theory, particularly those of Srinivasa Ramanujan, provide the foundation of a more simplified and unified view of the laws of nature than those of the "Standard Model" of quantum theory. Also, through these mathematical equations, we are able to deal with the strings collectively as one "Superstring."

At the heart of Superstring Theory lies the necessary principle of "self-consistency." In order for matter to exist, the string must resonate self-consistently (or, self-perpetually). Moreover, to do this, the laws of nature require the string to resonate not in four-dimensional space-time, but in ten dimensions—this is the source of the original ten-dimensional state of the universe.

Interestingly, another Greek philosopher and mathematician named Pythagoras (approximately one century before Anaxagoras) held the view that the universe, and everything in it, is "an organized structure of harmonics of resonance."

Additionally, Pythagoras discovered the numerical ratios underlying the intervals, which the Greeks called "consonants" and used as the basis of their musical scale. They involve only the numbers 1 to 4: 1:2, octave; 3:2, fifth, 4:3, fourth. Remarkably, these numbers add up to the number ten—a sacred number to the ancient Pythagoreans because it is "the source and root of everlasting nature."

Now that we have taken a closer look at the dynamics of matter, I find that I am compelled to ask a very critical question: what is the Superstring made of? Since it is the cause of the Super Resonance which waves matter into existence, where did the string derive the resonance which caused its existence?

Even if we turn a blind eye to the notion held by most physicists that the universe has a singularity (a beginning), or an "Arrow of Time," and, notwithstanding the concept that the string resonates "self-consistently," it still cannot have waved itself into existence—something else had to do the waving.

I have no problem with String Theory per se. But I find that String Theorists have brought a new set of old problems back into the arena of theories of existence. Their argument that the laws governing the conservation of energy and mass eliminates a beginning to the universe (and matter) are tautological and contradictory—particularly when they talk matter-of-factly about The Big Bang. Either it happened or it didn't happen. Either there was a beginning or there wasn't a beginning. Either time (in the physical universe) moves forward or it doesn't.

In his book *The City of God,* St. Augustine maintains that God exists outside of time, and that he created time for the sake of humanity. This raises another important issue. Since Einstein forever changed the way we think about space, didn't he also change the way we are to perceive time? But what kind of time are we talking about? The second law of thermodynamics (which String Theorists seem to conveniently ignore), along with the "Doppler Effect," provide the most compelling evidence that our universe has both a singularity (in The Big Bang) and an "Arrow of Time." This forward progression of time is unique only to our macroscopic universe—the universe in which living, physical beings exist.

The universe on the microscopic or quantum level, however, doesn't quite adhere to the same laws as our macro-universe. That's because, on the quantum level, time has no direction—this is what Stephen Hawking refers to as "imaginary time." It is no wonder that physicists enjoy working with mathematics expressed in "imaginary time" over "real time" because (as we shall see) time which has no direction eliminates pesky singularities.

But if God exists in a "super-dimension" outside of time, it must be independent of both "real" and "imaginary" time—it must, furthermore, be independent of space.

Yet, theoretical physics still likes to toy with the idea of a universe independent of God.

On this, Stephen Hawking offers an inciting perspective:

> **What is it that breathes fire into the equations and makes a universe for them to describe? Why does the universe go to all the bother of existing? Is the unified theory so compelling that it brings about its own existence? Or does it need a creator, and, if so, does he have an effect on the universe? And who created him?** (Hawking, 1988).

From a mathematical perspective, the Arrow of Time, coupled with the *c* constant of light, DO NOT HAPPEN BY RANDOM CHANCE—they are the most compelling evidence of the existence of a master "Creator" (only a Creator could come up with such stuff).

The problem confronting most theoretical physicists (especially String Theorists) is that they try to avoid singularities—and, therefore, a Creator—like the plague, because singularities are a perpetual source of "undesired" mathematical infinities. Theoretical physicists are seduced by the aesthetic beauty they see in mathematical equations which exclude infinities (and, therefore, singularities). The Nobel Prize winning physicist, Paul Dirac, commented: "It is more important to have beauty in one's equations than to have them fit the experiment." The theorists are trying to cleverly have it both ways, and, ultimately, that won't work.

This brings us back (again) to St. Thomas Aquinas. He was well aware that the true explanation of the origin of existence MUST TRANSCEND the old paradox of "which came first, the chicken or the egg?"

Despite our science and mathematics, our attempt to understand the sublime mystery, thus far, is frivolous at best. The matter ultimately runs deeper than anything we can imagine or comprehend. Regardless of how many directions we pursue, they all lead us back to the same point of inception—confronting the Divine Mystery.

Aquinas simply stated:

> **it is necessary to arrive at a first mover which is moved by no other—and this everyone understands to be God** (Aquinas, 1947–48).

God became "the first mover" when he created the Arrow of Time.

As we have already seen, Anaxagoras referred to the first mover as Mind. It really doesn't matter what words are used; they all describe the same process.

# 8

# HYPERDIMENSIONAL SYMMETRY

***Modern physics has definitely decided for Plato. For the smallest units of matter are, in fact, not physical objects in the ordinary sense of the word; they are forms, structures, or—in Plato's sense—Ideas, which can be unambiguously spoken of only in the language of mathematics.***

Werner Heisenberg

SINCE THE HYPERDIMENSION is really the confluence of all higher dimensions into *ONE* entity, why do we go to all the bother of distinguishing one from the other? The answer is that our brains are the product of space-time relationships. Thus, in order to understand the dynamics of *The Bigger Picture* we are compelled to view the characteristics of each higher dimensional *dynamic* individually, so that we may then realize its relationship to the rest. Perhaps the best way to understand this is to look at the way that space and time rotate into each other. As we have seen, space without time is meaningless. In fact, timeless space or spaceless time simply cannot exist. If time was not an integral aspect of space, we would be unable to distinguish one region of space from another—that is to say, that space which is farthest away would be indistinguishable from the space which is closest to us. Therefore, the interconnected relationship of space and time form the basis of the three spatial dimensions of width, depth, and height—with time as the fourth, space-time dimension.

Moreover, since the advent of *Relativity*, space can no longer be viewed as "emptiness." It has a material quality which is best described as a "fabric." However, the thread which runs throughout the fabric, giving it structure, is *time*.

The fabric of space-time explains a lot of things—it explains how space (in the presence of matter) can have curvature, and why light bends when traveling through curved regions of space. It may also explain why light appears to travel through space as a wave. Furthermore, the fabric of space-time offers a more precise understanding of how the hyper-gravity of *Black Holes* can warp space to form *Einstein Rosen Bridges* or *wormholes*. However, the concept of *tunneling* through the fabric of space to get to other *parallel universes* is meaningless unless we realize that parallel universes (if there are such things) are really separate regions of space which exist in distinctly different times or *world sheets*.

Since space-time assumes the physical characteristic of curvature, it is conceivable that it can also possess the quality of *wave function*. If we view space-time as a wave, in which space is the wave's crest and time is its trough, light traveling over the wave has little choice but conform to the wavy pattern—in which case, light merely appears to function as a wave. If this is true, the relationship between light and space-time engenders a more comprehensive understanding of how and why the "Arrow of Time" works.

Furthermore, if light conforms to the material characteristics of space-time (as it passes through space-time) it must necessarily conform to the laws, restrictions, and boundaries imposed by space-time. That is to say that light (functioning as a wave) assumes the quality of *moving* at the maximum velocity allowed within the confines of space-time. After all, the property of *movement* is unique only to space-time and is, therefore, subject to its own limitations.

During the summer of 2000, a group of physicists conducted an independent experiment in a laboratory in Princeton, New Jersey in which a pulse of laser light was beamed through a glass chamber filled with cesium vapor. The objective was to see if the light could be amplified by interacting with cesium atoms (an effect strikingly similar to the *Cerenkov condition*). Much to their amazement, the physicists found the light had already exited the chamber "before it had even finished entering." Proudly proclaiming a belief that they had conquered Relativity, the researchers claimed the interaction with the cesium atoms had caused the light to accelerate 310 times faster than its natural velocity of 186,000 miles per second.

Of course, the naïve assumptions drawn by the experimenters pose a multiplicity of problems. First, Relativity has never precluded the possibility that light can move faster than itself—it's just that the concept of light moving faster than itself is meaningless because no matter *what* we perceive or measure the speed of light to be, it is still the supreme, *constant* velocity. It is the *absolute* yardstick by which all other velocities in the material universe are measured, relative to how fast or slow time moves (according to various conditions). As a natural law, Relativity is not defined as much by the *movement* of light as it is defined by the limitations and variant nature of space-time, which in turn governs how things move. Moreover, since time is not absolute, the researchers should have considered a more probable explanation that time inside the chamber had actually slowed down, thus creating the perception that the light had accelerated. Second, the "distorted light" exiting the chamber had different properties than the light that was entering, therefore it was technically not the same light. And third, the researchers only observed the light entering and exiting the chamber. In other words, they didn't observe the light actually passing through the chamber's space. This is the most telling clue as to what really happened.

The researchers were, in fact, witnessing an interdimensional phenomenon. As the beam of light began its entrance, interacting with the cesium atoms, its properties of *movement* were altered—that is to say, it was pushed to the limit permitted by space-time. Upon reaching the limit, the space-time properties of the light dissolved, transforming it into *pure energy*. As pure energy, it was beyond space-time; it was hyperdimensional. In that instant, the pure energy took a detour in discontinuous time—only to re-emerge, instantaneously, on the other side of the chamber, with barely enough time to resume its space-time characteristics, thus appearing distorted. In theory, it is conceivable that the dynamics of light coming into contact with cesium atoms might be analogous to the dynamics of light entering a region of *quantum Black Holes*.

Whenever light enters anomalous regions of space such as *Black Holes*, it is pushed beyond the space-time threshold and is stripped of its space-time characteristics. True to form, theoretical physicists have traditionally dubbed this transcendental, paradoxical state of light as a *tachyon* (a quantum particle). Theoretically, tachyons are photons that have *transformed* into a state of *rest* (i.e., they don't move). However, tachyons, in ways not understood to physics, exist in a state which *appears* to exceed the *movement* or velocity of light.

In other words, contemporary physicists still haven't caught up with Thomas Aquinas. Aquinas maintained that light, in its purest form (angelic light), "can be now here and now there with no time interval in between ... but not in the way that bodily movements are." There is no movement *outside* space-time—and, as we have previously seen, Aquinas referred to this condition as *discontinuous movement*. Clearly, Aquinas understood Relativity in ways that continue to elude present-day physicists. Furthermore, he saw that *pure energy* is hyperdimensional—that is to say, *energy* which conforms to the confines of space-time translates into *pure, spiritual energy* when it TRANSCENDS space-time.

The concept of hyperdimensional reality is not new. It began with some of the greatest physicists of the nineteenth century—most notably, Georg Bernhard Riemann, Sir William Thompson, James Clerk Maxwell, and Sir William Rowan Hamilton. Utilizing a higher dimensional, "numerological" form of mathematics called *quaternions* (devised by Sir William Hamilton), James Clerk Maxwell was able to demonstrate that electricity and magnetism rotate into each other as one, unified entity—electromagnetism.

Quaternions are actually a simple version of what modern physicists now refer to as *gauge symmetry*. Gauge symmetry is a system of mathematically shuffling or rotating objects (which do not ordinarily appear to have a symmetrical relationship) so that the (hidden) manner in which they are symmetrically aligned with one another is *revealed*. Whenever this happens, the objects can be seen as being *unified*. Gauge symmetry is not a trick. It is a higher dimensional dynamic which shows us the true, unified nature of things which are otherwise not evident when viewed from a lower-dimensional perspective. Gauge symmetry forms the mathematical backbone of *quantum electrodynamic theory, quantum chromodynamic theory*, and *superstring theory*. In fact, if it were not for gauge symmetry, we would not be enjoying many of the modern electrical conveniences we so easily take for granted.

Throughout the latter part of the nineteenth century, the rudiments of hyperdimensional physics were quite contagious. In 1867, Sir William Thompson (later known as Baron Kelvin of Largs) took a hyperdimensional approach to the very nature of atomic structure. He proposed that material existence wasn't comprised of particle atoms at all. Instead, Thompson hypothesized a universe pervaded by a network of "vortex atoms," each infinitesimal in size, and having the characteristics of "self-sustaining" (or self-consistent) "whirlpools." Moreover, the vortex atom possessed the property of elasticity. Thompson, in a crude way, was undoubtedly predicting the existence of the Superstring.

With the turning of the twentieth century, Einstein realized that Maxwell's brilliant but extensive equations lacked a critical piece of the puzzle. While demonstrating the unity of electricity and magnetism, Maxwell had completely overlooked the unity of space and time. As a result, his equations were extremely long and tedious. So, in one master stroke, Einstein (in unifying space and time) reduced Maxwell's voluminous equations down to one simple equation. Through the simplicity of higher dimensions, Special Relativity was born.

One of the reasons the higher dimensional mathematics of quaternions became obscure is due, in part, to an unfortunate connection with the prevailing notion (in the late nineteenth century) that the hyperdimension WAS the fourth, higher dimension. Einstein, of course, shattered that idea. However, Hamilton's original, concept of quaternions (which are, numerologically, symmetrical *pairs* of "real numbers" which are added or multiplied in accordance with specific rules) was not without merit.

As we shall see in Chapter 20, the brilliant, highly enigmatic Sarah Winchester (a woman whose life spanned both the nineteenth and twentieth centuries) achieved an ingenious method of synthesizing a highly advanced blend of quaternions, gauge symmetry, and Superstring theory into *one*, hyperdimensional numerology. Winchester saw the hidden symmetry inherent in the relationship of all numbers. She further saw that numbers are a higher dimension unto themselves. Moreover, numbers possess a mystical quality of intuitive revelation—that is to say, persons following the guidance of their intuitive faculties are irresistibly drawn to numbers as higher dimensional beacons leading the way to insight into the true transcendental nature of the hyperdimension. All things in the material and spiritual universe are intricately related through the unifying power of numbers.

# 9

# THE ANTHROPIC PRINCIPLE

***Did God have any choice in creating the universe?***

Albert Einstein

***God does not play dice!***

Albert Einstein

IT IS CLEAR THAT along with a more refined and deeper understanding of existence comes a profoundly more refined and deeper understanding of its divine source. Indeed, the latest scientific discoveries about our universe, over the past few decades, have resulted in an ever expanding body of evidence which leads us to the irresistible conclusion that our universe didn't just happen by random chance.

In fact, physicists are now compelled to acknowledge that there is a vast symmetry to the universe in which an infinite number of constants, values, and ratios had to be satisfied with absolute precision in order to come into existence the way that it has—intricately designed for the existence of life. For example, the slightest deviation in the relationship of the gravitational force to the force of electromagnetism would have produced a universe devoid of life-giving stars such as our sun. Or, had the strength of the strong nuclear force been lessened in the slightest degree, our universe would be made only of hydrogen, precluding all other elements and compounds, most notably, water, oxygen, and carbon—all essential to life. Moreover, the smallest variation of the dynamics of the strong nuclear force, the weak nuclear force, the electromagnetic force, or gravity would have given us a universe with an unlimited number of hostile scenarios; e.g., a universe without stars, or a universe without atoms, or a universe made entirely of helium, or, a universe which would have imploded back into itself immediately following The Big Bang. The list of possible divergent universes is endless.

In light of these truths, the scientific community has come to recognize a most compelling principle of the laws governing our universe:

1. The universe is uniquely designed for the existence of life.
2. Such a design had to have already been at work at the moment of The Big Bang.

This scientific maxim is known as "The Anthropic Principle." In other words, our universe COULD NOT have arisen from nothing, nor COULD IT have emerged from chaos. From the first instant of its inception (or conception), it came into existence CONFORMING to a precise, symmetrical design. This can only be the result of an INTELLIGENCE that knows exactly WHAT it is doing, and WHY it is doing it! I have found that scientists and mathematicians alike generally ascribe to the notion that our universe is the product of such an INTELLIGENCE; they just bicker about how to describe it (depending on their cultural, religious, or spiritual agenda). Some call it THE ORGANIZING PRINCIPLE, some call it the SOURCE, some call it THE CREATOR—but, for the most part, those who recognize the transcendent nature of the INTELLIGENCE, prefer to call it GOD.

Aquinas simply referred to GOD as the *first mover.* In order that the first mover be moved by no other, Aquinas recognized that God had to exist in "discontinuous time"—the "eternal now." This is an essential element which distinguishes the dimension of Spirit from the dimensions of space-time.

Since the existence of matter requires the presence of space-time, and vice versa, the resonance which creates matter originates in the hyperdimension which transcends space-time.

Thus, the source of the "Super Resonance" is a result of what Aquinas refers to as "discontinuous movement," or, put another way, it is an activity of pure thought, created by the Divine Mind. Therefore, the hyperdimension emerges purely as the Dimension of Mind and Spirit—the ultimate, transcendent state of existence.

Another scientific precept called "Ockham's Razor" states that "all things being equal, the simplest answer is the true one." So, all things being equal, the Divine Mind reveals itself as the ultimate source of everything, and, simply *manifests* all things into existence, through discontinuous movement ... in discontinuous time.

It has been said that Einstein wanted to know the mind of God, and, that he would, on occasion, talk of angels. No doubt, they were talking to him. They were most certainly the same angels who talked with Aquinas, Anaxagoras, and Pythagoras ... in the hyperdimension.

# 10

# THE DREAMGATE
## *Window to the Hyperdimension*

*All that we see or seem*
*Is but a dream within a dream.*

Edgar Allan Poe

*But I, being poor, have only my dreams;*
*I have spread my dreams under your feet;*
*Tread softly because you tread on my dreams.*

William Butler Yeats

### The Psychic Connection

OF ALL THE PHYSIOLOGICAL PHENOMENA of the human body studied by modern science, sleep is the least understood. It is a vital function. We all have to sleep just as surely as we have to eat and breathe. But, until recent history, nobody had a clue as to why we have to sleep.

Early in the twentieth century, the famed Russian physiologist and psychologist, Ivan Pavlov, acknowledged that for some unexplained reason, the brain, on a daily basis, seemed to *require* a "tuned down" state, resulting in sleep. But why? The answer is that sleep is prerequisite to the attainment of the dream state.

In the early 1950s, a team of researchers, Dr. Nathan Kleitman, and a graduate student, Eugene Aserinski, working at the University of Chicago, began studying the rapid eye movement of human subjects during sleep. Much to their amazement, Kleitman and Aserinski found that, invariably, upon waking a subject during a rapid-eye movement (REM) episode, the subject would report being immersed in a dream. Thus, modern dream research was born.

In the years that have followed, scientific researchers have concluded that it is not really the sleep that we need, rather it is the dreaming. We all have to dream.

As a rule, we need to dream at least once every twenty-four hours. In fact, the maximum threshold of REM deprivation anyone can tolerate without suffering harmful effects is set at around seventy-two hours. Whenever we are deprived of REM sleep, it must be restored in an amount exactly equivalent to that which was lost. Our dreams cannot be compromised. Loss of non-REM sleep, however, does not have to be recovered.

So, why do we have to dream? Some scientists have attempted to explain dreaming as being nothing more than a neuro-chemical process in which the brain rids itself of non-essential information it has processed during its daily operation—and some psychologists have dismissed dreams as mere "fantasy" and "wishful thinking." Such explanations not only lack scientific merit, but they totally ignore the spiritual side of the matter. The proponents of this atavistic, mechanized view of life are oblivious to the question, "what is the soul doing when the body is shut down in sleep?" Clearly, the soul has no need of sleep.

Speaking from personal experience, I can say that, so long as we exist in the physical realm, the dream state is, in fact, the direct window through which we have access with the hyperdimension.

Dreaming is an essential activity of the soul—it is our psychic connection with the Divine Mind. All ancient cultures and civilizations understood this psychic connection between the dream state and Divinity. The ancient Egyptians, Greeks, Romans, and Chinese—the Aborigines, and the Native Americans all saw the dimension of dreams as a real place where the soul would nightly sojourn to commune with spirit guides, and receive valuable information and insight.

The process of dreaming is one of transformation. Since it is impossible for our physical bodies to connect with the hyperdimension, the soul, quite literally, disengages from the body when it goes about the business of dreaming.

Angels are always present in the dream state—a fact the dreamer may not always be aware of, or remember. Since angels do not have form, their communication with us is telepathic. Also, the language of angels is symbolic. They speak to us in symbols. This is why upon awaking, our recollection of a dream often seems to be a jumble of gibberish and confused images which have no conscious or worldly meaning.

The world-renowned psychologist Carl Gustav Jung said:

> **God speaks chiefly through dreams and visions... In dreams, symbols occur spontaneously, for dreams happen and are not invented; they are, therefore, the main source of all our knowledge about symbolism. ... This is what 'dream language' does; its symbolism has so much psychic energy that we are forced to pay attention to it** (Jung, 1964).

Because dreaming takes place in the hyperdimension, most of what we are experiencing is completely ineffable—there are simply no words sufficient enough to describe higher dimensions. This is the domain of pure thought. Neither time nor space, nor physical objects exist there.

From the dreamer's perspective, the duration of the dream and the sequence of the "dream events" have no relevance. Dream events have a remarkable way of happening all at once over an indefinite period—at the speed of thought. This is the essence of discontinuous time—it is the eternal now. Thus, when we wake from our dreams, our recollection of dream events has no time gauge.

In Chapter 1, I spoke of my childhood, and my nightly dream excursions to what I called "The Place of Mirrors and Light." Despite the inadequacy of the description, it was the best I could provide. In the years that followed my near-death experience, I came to realize that the mirrors were really my interpretation of how everything appears from the perspective of higher dimensions, and still words can never describe it.

Then too, came the realization that the ever-present, brilliant light is the essence of pure thought—again, mere words cannot describe the transcendent beauty, love, and understanding I have always felt when in the presence of that light.

Dreams are one of the most significant aspects of our lives—they're our implements of insight, our dynamic theater of enlightenment. The more we cultivate our dreams, the more we understand and grow.

The ancient Egyptians and Greeks practiced "dream incubation." This is a process in which, prior to sleep, one meditates about a specific issue or problem which needs to be resolved, or in which greater insight is needed—in so doing, the dream becomes focused on the specific issue.

About 50% of our dreaming is spent working on spiritual development. When we awake from these dreams, we usually remember little or nothing about them—this is because such dreams are completely symbolic and have little to do with the physical realm.

Another aspect of our dreaming is spent solving problems or overcoming barriers which disrupt the progress of our daily lives. In these dreams, we generally experience highly symbolic dream events which do not seem to make sense in the temporal world. For example, we might find ourselves in unfamiliar places. Or, we might interact with people we don't recognize, or interact with people we used to know in the distant past, or people who are deceased. "Acting out" in symbolic imagery helps us to constructively deal with problematic situations or with hidden agendas.

There are, however, dreams which are explicitly directed to bring us highly detailed information. These are revelatory dreams. Their purpose is to intervene in our lives, or, in some cases, the lives of others. Angels are always the messengers who bring us such revelations. The pages of history are filled with accounts of dream revelations which have dramatically altered the course of human affairs.

Whenever a revelation occurs, the dreamer, upon awaking, always knows the exact purpose of the revelation.

Elias Howe's invention of the sewing machine came to him in a revelatory dream. Albert Einstein's Theory of Relativity was the result of dream revelation. In fact, he maintained that all of his life's work was the product of recurring continuations of the same dream. The concept of atomic structure was revealed to Niels Bohr in a dream, the result of which earned him the Nobel Prize. The turning point in the life of the French mathematician and philosopher, Rene Descartes, occurred during a dream in which an angel revealed to him mathematical concepts which have had a profound impact on the development of Western science. All of the mathematical equations of Srinivasa Ramanujan were, he said, the result of his spirit guide revealing the equations to him in recurring dreams throughout his life. These are the mathematical equations of higher dimensions which form the foundation of modern String Theory in theoretical physics.

Since dreaming is an inter-dimensional activity, it should be clear that the cultivation of our dreams is really a matter of cultivating our relationship with our angel guides. Remember, we have to invite them in—it's a give-and-take relationship.

Angels are not only our guides and guardians, they are, in a sense, our teachers. They are the intermediaries between the Divine Mind and us. Through dreams we have direct access with their domain. It is up to each of us to choose how we use it.

# 11

# PROPHETIC DREAMING

***All men of action are dreamers.***

James G. Hunekar

***Thou dost make possible things not so held,***
***Communicat'st with dreams.***

William Shakespeare

PROPHETIC DREAMING is revelatory and interventional—it is also pre-cognitive and visionary. The Bible is abundant with accounts of prophecy arising from angelic intervention through dreams. Perhaps the most salient prophetic episode of the Bible is in the book of Revelation. In his apocalyptic narrative, John speaks to us from a visionary dream in which he is visited by many angels (the word angel appears seventy times throughout the narrative). However, it is one principal angel who speaks to John with absolute authority—with a "voice like a trumpet;" e.g., "Write on a scroll what you see. ... Do not be afraid. ...

Come up here, and I will show you what must take place after this" (Revelation 1:10-11, 17; 4:1). The angel proceeds to show John a long procession of future eschatological events.

Not all prophetic dreams are as forceful as John's apocalyptic vision. In most cases, prophetic dreaming is much more subtle. For example:

> **a word was secretly brought to me, my ears caught a whisper of it. Amid disquieting dreams in the night, when deep sleep falls on men ... a spirit glided past my face ... a form stood before my eyes, and I heard a hushed voice"** (Job 4:12-13, 15-16).

Most prophetic dreams are directed to the dreamer for the purpose of intervening in the lives of others. When this happens, it is because the person for whom the intervention is intended simply is not tuned in to the angelic voices in the night. A prophetic dream was directed to Julius Caesar's wife, Cornelia, who warned him of the impending disaster awaiting him on the steps of the Roman Senate. Needless to say, his resultant assassination is a classic case of failure to heed.

One of the most remarkable examples of prophecy intervening in the lives of thousands of people can be found in the life of the late psychic and "religious seer," Edgar Cayce.

As a child, Cayce began to experience dream visions. In some cases, his visions put him in contact with deceased relatives.

As his life progressed, Cayce's psychic capacity, emanating from prophetic dream episodes, expanded to such a heightened state, that he was able to diagnose the medical conditions of people whom he had never met.

"The sleeping prophet," as he was called, helped more than 8,000 people throughout the United States over a period of forty-three years—most of these people had ailments which medical doctors were unable to diagnose.

Doctors from all over the country, being aware of Cayce's amazing gift, needed only to provide him with a patient's name and address, whereupon Cayce would go into a trance-like dream state and connect with the patient (regardless of the physical distance between them). Upon awaking, Cayce would write down a detailed and incredibly accurate diagnosis of the patient's medical malady.

In 1954 (nine years after Cayce's death), the University of Chicago awarded a Ph.D. for a doctoral dissertation chronicling Cayce's extraordinary life and work.

# 12

# THE KIRLIAN EFFECT
## *Traces of the Nonorganic Life Force*

***Nature shows us only the tail of the lion. But I do not doubt that the lion belongs to it even though he cannot at once reveal himself because of his enormous size.***

Albert Einstein

IN 1949, the husband and wife team of Semyon and Valentina Kirlian set out to demonstrate the existence of a "ghostlike" form of energy which both permeates and surrounds the living physical body. Using a "high frequency," high voltage form of photography they had just invented (and which bears their name), they were able to capture trace images of the high frequency energy on film.

As scientists began to speculate about the far reaching implications of this "life-force" energy, they sought to put a label on it: "corona discharge, aura, biological plasma body," etc. I personally find this to be interesting in light of the fact that for thousands of years the Chinese have called the same life-force energy Chi'i, and, in India, it has always been called Prana.

By the late 1960's, Russian scientists from the Kirov State University of Kazakhstan in Alma-Alta were studying the "Kirlian Phenomenon" under an electron microscope—a process reminiscent of the techniques used by laboratory physicists to photograph the tell-tale traces of activity generated by the collision of invisible quarks in experiments involving the splitting of atoms. While observing living organisms through the Kirlian high frequency discharge, the Russians discovered the trace activity of the organism's non-organic component. In other words, they were witnessing the tell-tale evidence of a spiritual body double.

Not surprisingly, the Soviet government thrust Kirlian research into top secret status. Such was the case for more than twenty years.

Notwithstanding Soviet efforts to keep a lid on Kirlian technology (particularly from Western observers), Semyon and Valentina Kirlian continued their research. Most notably, they discovered that the missing portion of a mutilated leaf, which was not visible in regular photographs, suddenly became eerily visible in "electrophotographs" using their technique. This is now known as the "phantom leaf effect."

Harold A. Widdison, a prominent researcher in near death experience, states:

> **The phantom leaf effect suggests the possibility that living organisms may be composed both of a**

> **biological component (which can be photographed using the conventional technique) and a nonbiological component (which can be photographed only when the Kirlian technique is used).**
>
> **This technological advance poses questions. ... Do living organisms have both a biological and nonbiological component? If there are two components, must they coexist or can one component exist without the other? If one can exist only in conjunction with the other, then why does the Kirlian photograph differ from the conventional photograph? If the nonbiological component, or "life force," can function independently of the biological component, can the life force exist separately in another dimension? If there is another dimension which coexists with the physical dimension, then is it possible that, as an individual approaches death, his state of consciousness is altered so that he gains glimpses of that other dimension?** (Widdison, 1982).

Widdison's terse questions engender compelling and profound answers. However, since he and others involved in the study of Kirlian technology seem reticent to include the term "soul," allow me to do so. Let's not mince words—terms such as "nonbiological component, life force, Chi'i, Prana, and soul" all refer to the same life energy.

Moreover, the energy of the soul includes consciousness and thought. It also includes the "astral body." Our astral body is the spiritual double of our physical body. It resonates at extremely high frequencies. It is, in fact, the discharge of the astral body's resonance that Kirlian technology images on film.

# 13

# OUT-OF-BODY EXPERIENCE (OBE) AND ASTRAL PROJECTION

*Wavering between the profit and the loss*
*In this brief transit where the dreams cross*
*The dreamcrossed twilight between birth and dying.*

T.S. Elliot

When we enter the "dreamgate," our astral body disengages from the physical body and the physical dimension of space-time, and instantly engages the hyper-dimension much like a transference of thought. Many people, while dreaming, experience the sensation of astral projection; i.e., separating from their physical bodies—floating, as it were, to some other place or perspective.

In 1966, Dr. Charles Tart, professor emeritus of psychology at the University of California at Davis, conducted a series of out-of-body experiments. In Tart's most famous experiment, specially recruited subjects whose dreams typically involved OBE's would sleep in a control room specifically designed for the experiment. On a small shelf, just inches from the control room ceiling, Tart would place a piece of paper on which was written a five-digit number known only to himself. Additionally, he would change the number on a daily basis. The subjects were carefully monitored. Amazingly, upon awaking, the subjects would recount their experience of astrally projecting out of their bodies to a vantage point where they could observe the five digit number. With nearly 100% accuracy they were able to disclose the five digit numbers to the researchers.

That same year, Dr. Stanley Krippner, professor of psychology and director of The Dream Laboratory at Maimonides Medical Center in Brooklyn, New York, read about Tart's OBE research. Impressed with both Tart's results and the inability of skeptics to refute his findings, Krippner took up the torch and began reproducing the experiment. In lieu of Tart's five-digit numbers, Krippner used pictures. The results were identical to Tart's.

Krippner and his colleagues went further. They studied subjects who were "telepathic dreamers." One dreamer would be "the receiver" while another would be "the sender"—both would be locked away in separate rooms.

Prior to entering into an REM cycle, the sender would look at a picture which had been randomly selected from a field of hundreds of different pictures all sealed in envelopes. Upon awaking, the receiver would accurately describe the key elements of the picture the sender had observed before dreaming. From 1966 to 1972 thousands of such experiments took place.

The work of Tart and Krippner ostensibly inspired a new field of psychic dream investigation called "remote viewing." In this technique a trained "viewer" goes into a trance-like dream state, accessing the hyperdimension.

Through remote viewing, things which cannot be perceived in four-dimensional space-time suddenly become perceivable from the perspective of higher dimensions. The viewer can see all things regardless of where they are and when they are. In other words, a viewer can observe all things from all vantage points simultaneously—this includes viewing everything in the past, present, and future tense.

For decades, during the cold war, the United States Army and the Soviet KGB poured millions upon millions of dollars into their respective top secret remote viewing programs—each hoping to achieve the upper hand in the ultimate act of espionage. To this day, the envelope of secrecy remains tightly sealed.

As we shall see in Chapter 14, remote viewing is far from being the utmost state of consciousness. There are still many levels which transcend our mortal reach.

Emanuel Swedenborg saw little distinction between the astral body's relationship with the hyperdimension through the dreamgate, and its relationship through death—he referred to the astral body as the "interior soul" or the "interior man." Swedenborg observed:

> **With regard to the soul, of which it is said it shall live after death, it is nothing else than the man himself, who lives in the body, that is, the interior man, who by the body acts in the world, and who**

> **gives to the body to live; this man, when he is loosed from the body, is called a spirit, and appears then altogether in human form, yet cannot in any wise be seen by the eyes of the body, but by the eyes of the spirit** (Swedenborg 1854).

Since the purpose of dreaming is to gain access to the hyperdimension, it is, in a sense, analogous with death.

It is no wonder that many Chinese, to this very day, have an aversion to alarm clocks for fear their dreaming souls might be prematurely shut out of their physical bodies. Frightening though that thought may be, it need not be so. For dreaming, although essential to our development as human beings, only gives us fleeting glimpses through the spirit windows of the hyperdimension. The supreme state of consciousness awaits us only when we have "shuffled off this mortal coil."

# 14

# NEAR-DEATH EXPERIENCE

*All say, "How hard it is that we have to die"—*
*a strange complaint to come from the mouths of people*
*who have had to live.*

Mark Twain

*I don't mind dying. I just don't*
*want to be there when it happens!*

Woody Allen

DEEP DOWN INSIDE the consciousness of all humans (even, I suspect, the consciousness of atheists) there lies, at some level, the primal intuition that the act of living doesn't end with the act of dying.

I can attest to the fact that the experience of dying or being near death takes us to a level of hyperdimensional consciousness which is vastly deeper and more profound than anything we can experience in the dreamgate—although it is true that as long as there have been humans, the transition of death and the transition of dreams have always been compared to each other. Yet, death remains the ultimate transcendent experience.

So, "What is it like to die?" This is the first question posed by Dr. Raymond A. Moody, Jr., in his remarkable book *Life After Life.* For decades, Moody has been asking this question of hundreds of people who, like me, have been there.

Of course Moody has not been the first or the only person involved in near-death research—there are many others. What is most interesting is that nearly all NDE researchers, after years of scientific investigation, have come to a startling discovery. While studying people who had been pronounced clinically dead, and then were later resuscitated, regardless of their national, cultural, socio-economic, religious and nonreligious backgrounds, the researchers were reporting virtually identical information about the informant's glimpses into the afterlife.

How could so many divergent people, under such extraordinary circumstances, who had never met one another, separated geographically by thousands of miles, have shared the same experiences? To all of us who have shared in the experience, the answer is obvious—we have all entered the exquisite level of existence in the hyper-dimension that is the afterlife—only to be sent rushing back to our physical bodies.

Moody went on to construct a composite model which includes all of the various "common elements" of NDEs:

> **A man is dying, and, as he reaches the point of greatest physical distress, he hears himself pro-**

nounced dead by his doctor. He begins to hear an uncomfortable noise, a loud ringing or buzzing, and at the same time feels himself moving very rapidly through a long dark tunnel. After this, he suddenly finds himself outside of his own physical body ... he sees his own body from a distance, as though he is a spectator. He watches the resuscitation attempt from this unusual vantage point and is in a state of emotional upheaval.

After a while, he collects himself. ... He notices that he still has a "body" but one of a very different nature and with very different powers from the physical body he has left behind. Soon other things begin to happen. ... He glimpses the spirits of relatives and friends who have already died, and a loving, warm spirit of a kind he has never encountered before—a being of light—appears before him. This being asks him a question, nonverbally, to make him evaluate his life and helps him along by showing him a panoramic, instantaneous playback of the major events of his life ... he finds himself approaching some sort of barrier or border, apparently representing the limit between earthly life and the next life. Yet, he finds that he must go back to the earth. ... At this point he resists, for now he is taken up with his experiences in the afterlife and does not want to return. He is overwhelmed by intense feelings of joy, love, and peace. Despite his attitude, though, he somehow reunites with his physical body and lives.

Later he tries to tell others ... he can find no human words adequate to describe these unearthly episodes. He also finds that others scoff, so he stops telling other people. Still, the experience affects his

> **life profoundly, especially his views about death and its relationship to life** (Moody, 1982).

Not all of the elements of the Moody model are experienced by everyone who has been through an NDE. For example, I didn't encounter any deceased relatives or friends during my near-death experience. One thing is certain, the similarities of the experience far outweigh the dissimilarities.

Virtually everyone who has had a near-death experience reports the feeling of detachment from their physical body, and the sense of being in their astral body.

Also, the experience of viewing one's physical body from an other-dimensional vantage point is quite common, along with the sensation of passing or rushing through a long dark tunnel—then, there is always the Being of Light. For me the Being of Light was not unusual, as I was already used to the presence of angel guides.

However, the panoramic life review was a new twist for me. What is most interesting about the life review is that every one of us who has experienced it gets the clear impression that the angel guide was in no way judgmental, but rather showed complete love, caring, and understanding.

Another universal aspect of NDEs is the realization that the experience is happening in a higher dimensional realm—that it transcends space and time, and that it is blissfully beyond the scope of words to describe. The psychologist Carl Jung, while suffering a heart attack in 1944, had a near-death experience. Jung stated:

> **The images were so tremendous that I myself concluded that I was close to death... I had the feeling that everything was being sloughed away;**

> **everything I had aimed at or wished for or thought, the whole phantasmagoria of earthly existence, fell away or was stripped from me. ... Nevertheless something remained; it was as if I now carried along with me everything I had ever experienced or done, everything that had happened around me. ... I consisted of all that, so to speak. I consisted of my own history, and I felt with great certainty: this is what I am. I am this bundle of what has been and what has been accomplished. ... I existed in an objective form; I was what I had been and lived. ... I would never have imagined that such experience was possible. It was not a product of my imagination. The visions and experiences were utterly real; there was nothing subjective about them; they all had the quality of absolute objectivity. ... I felt as though I were floating in space, as though I were safe in the womb of the universe—in a tremendous void, but filled with the highest possible feeling of happiness. ...**
>
> **I can describe the experience only as the ecstasy of a non-temporal state in which present, past, and future are one. Everything that happens in time had been brought together into a concrete whole. Nothing was distributed over time, nothing could be measured by temporal concepts. ... "This is eternal bliss," I thought. This cannot be described; it is far too wonderful** (Jung, 1961).

Jung's account typifies the acute consciousness of discontinuous time in NDEs accompanied by the inability to find words sufficient to describe the experience, and the implicit understanding that the transcendental state of the afterlife is the domain of mind and pure thought.

One of my clients who was resuscitated after being thrown from his car in a nearly fatal car accident reports:

> **I knew I was dead. I had no physical or sensory consciousness. It was clear that my mind and my thoughts were all that remained. Time didn't pass in the way that it does on earth. There was only the now which didn't seem to change or move in any direction. I was in a place where only my mind mattered—space didn't exist. Feelings of love and peacefulness had no limit there. It was like nothing I had ever experienced before, and as I'm talking about it now, there's just no way I can come close to describing it the way it actually was.**

The universal element of encountering a Being of Light who exhibits a panoramic "life review" is quite remarkable. Nearly all of those who have reported NDEs give vivid accounts of such encounters. The experience invariably describes meeting or being drawn to a brilliant light, brighter and uniquely different from any other light. The light has a distinct personality and communicates with the person who is near death. The communication is never verbal, there is absolutely no language involved—it occurs as a clear and perfect transfer of thought. In fact, the communication is so perfect that misunderstanding or lying is impossible.

Another important aspect of the encounter is that the Being of Light has a divine purpose. Because there is no language involved, words like God and angel are not evident. However, it is crystal clear to the person experiencing near death that the Being of Light is there to guide, guard, and love. This is the point where the life review is usually manifested.

What is especially significant about the life review is that the angel guide (Being of Light) seems to use the review as a means of getting the person, who is passing over, to reflect on the effect of each event of their life. As this is happening, the angel guide asks deliberative yet non-judgmental questions such as "are you pleased with what you have done?" And, "was it worth it?" Or, "are you ready to pass over?"

One person who had been through a near-death experience told me:

> **It was as if these angels were helping me to assess my life in such a way that I would instantly be able to decide whether or not I had learned or accomplished all that I had been in the world to do. Love seemed to be a big issue. Everything I had done or even thought was, somehow, the result of my love or lack of love, and, some way, this was all tied into the level of learning I had achieved. I was really having fun; my angel guide had a pleasant sense of humor. He would say things like, "well, it looks like you really blew it there." It was like he already knew the answers, but I had to know the answers, and then make a choice.**

It should be emphasized that in all of the NDEs (involving an encounter with a Being of Light) which have been reported, the Being of Light is always completely loving, understanding, and compassionate beyond anything experienced in earthly existence.

Another element of near-death experience is what Dannion Brinkley, in his book *Saved By the Light,* calls "the boxes of knowledge" or "the hall of knowledge." This usually occurs after the life review. In some cases, like Brinkley's, the person who is near death experiences drifting or floating into a kind of city or cathedral of beautiful lights—it is here that one is imbued with a complete and total knowingness, a perfect knowledge of everything. It is intuition in its highest and most pristine form. My experience didn't include seeing the city of lights, but it did involve the perfect knowingness when the powerful telepathic voice said "understand." The feeling of that moment was, and still is, totally beyond description.

After the life review and the knowingness, the angel guide directs one's attention to a sort of barrier or symbolic line of demarcation—what is communicated here gives one a clear understanding that this is where one realm ends and another begins—to cross over means there is no coming back. This is usually the point when the person near death is sent rushing back to their physical body in the temporal world.

Another person, who had suffered a heart attack, reported:

> **It was like the lights went out for a moment. I knew I was no longer in my physical body, I felt like I was flying through a dark void. I thought God, so this is it, I'm dead. Then I saw a fantastic light, it kept getting brighter, it had the most beautiful golden color like nothing I'd never seen. This light started talking to me but without words. It was like it knew my thoughts and I knew its thoughts. It**

> **made me look at my whole life, almost like watching my life as if it was a movie, except it was the real deal, it was every single moment of my life in 3D, but it was happening all at once. I can't really describe it. I saw a lot of things I wish I could go back and undo or redo.**
>
> **I remember thinking this is no dream, this is all real—and clear, I mean it was all much clearer than things are in the ordinary world. There was also this bluish almost grayish fog, I could see what looked like human forms on the other side of the fog. I thought, do I know these people? As I looked over their heads and I could see what must have been buildings, they seemed to be made of a kind of beautiful crystal that shined with an iridescent light. I wanted to go there. As I approached, an incredible feeling of love and joy came over me, everything was so peaceful, there is just no way to describe how I felt. Then, suddenly, I saw my mother, clear as day, on the other side of the fog. She looked at me saying, "I know you want to come over here, but you're not ready yet. You still have much to do with your life." No sooner did I start to tell her how much I wanted to stay then I found myself instantly back in my body.**

An additional point to be made is that NDEs have a heightened clarity about them that transcends our thoughts and perceptions in the temporal realm. It is not the same as the dream state.

I find it interesting that a disciplined psychoanalyst like Carl Jung, after experiencing near death, stated, emphatically, "I would never have imagined that such an experience was possible. It was not a product of my imagination. The visions and experiences were utterly real; there was nothing subjective about them; they all had the quality of absolute objectivity." Ironically, had one of Jung's patients come to him with such an account a few years earlier, Jung, the scientist, would no doubt have written it off as being completely subjective, "archetypal" thinking.

A number of years ago an acquaintance of mine said, "if everything is so wonderful when we die, why don't we all just commit suicide so we can get there sooner?" Over the years I have talked with a number of people who have gone the suicide route. Their experiences were not pretty.

The problem is that whatever baggage we create in life goes with us into the next phase of our existence. Not only does the selfish act of suicide fail to solve anything, but it just compounds and perpetuates the misery that was already present.

We are all here to learn important spiritual lessons, particularly lessons about love. Suicide is one of the ultimate acts of hatred. It is hatred toward oneself, and it is hatred towards the divinity that resides within the self—it is the exact opposite of what we are all here to do. So, it is not surprising to hear people who have been near death through suicide, talk not of a peaceful, tranquil afterlife, but instead, they talk of experiencing something rather like a kind of hell or limbo.

One of these people told me:

**I had lost my job and my husband. It seemed as if I had lost everything. I hated my life. I'm not a religious person, so I said screw it, I'm outta here. I**

**filled the bathtub full of warm water, got in and pulled out a razor blade. As I cut my wrists open I noticed there wasn't much pain, the real pain would soon be over.**

**The bath water was getting red with blood and I was getting dizzy and faint. I floated out of my body and just looked down at myself laying there in the tub. Then I realized I was dead. That was a shock. I had hoped I was just going to go to sleep and that would be the end.**

**Everything turned black. I was no longer floating, it's more like I was flying through a dark vacuum. Eventually, I came to a sudden stop. I was still in this dark place, it was like being in some kind of suspended animation. I could see lights far off in a distance; they seemed to be thousands of miles away. I knew I was going to be in this place a long time. I was so alone. This was the loneliest I had ever been. I just kept thinking, how could I have done this to myself? I could see now that it wasn't my place to take my life, that life is a gift. I wished I hadn't done it.**

**Then, I found myself laying in a bed in the hospital; I had been revived. I was fortunate; my girlfriend had found my body and called the paramedics. Now I have a second chance to get it right this time."**

The reader should know that I am, in no way, casting moral aspersions or being judgmental about suicide. There are many different situations which can bring a person to commit the act. Suffice it to say, however, that of all the wise choices we can make in life, suicide it is clearly not one of them. Just as there is a cause for every effect, so there is a consequence for every action.

As we shall see (in the coming chapters), once a person's soul takes permanent leave of its physical body, and crosses over into the hyperdimension, it is not barred from returning to the physical realm. The process of spiritual development continues.

# PART THREE

# COMMUNICATING WITH THE DECEASED

# 15

# TRANSITIONAL LESSONS

*There is no Death! What seems so is transition;*
*This life of mortal breath*
*Is but a suburb of the life elysian,*
*Whose portal we call death.*

Henry Wadsworth Longfellow

*Behold—not him we knew!*
*This was the prison which his soul looked through.*

Oliver Wendell Holmes

JUST AS THERE ARE LAWS which govern the workings of the physical universe, so too there are laws which govern the dynamics of the spiritual universe. The human spirit is, in essence, assigned to implement creative deeds in an amazingly circumscribed, physical world that is both stifling and full of ungainly obstacles.

Our one true freedom in our temporal lives is the freedom of choice. We can choose to create loving actions, the result of which glorifies all that is divine, or we can choose to commit selfish, indifferent, loveless acts resulting in the destruction of the human spirit—this is the basis of our evolving or devolving as spiritual beings.

For all intents and purposes, our earthly existence is our proving ground. Spiritual law reveals that all things happen for a purpose—the experience of near death is no exception.

During his near-death experience, upon realizing that he was being sent back to his physical body, Carl Jung compared existing in space-time to being bound within the confines of a prison. On this, Jung said:

> **Disappointed, I thought, now I must return to the "box system" again. For it seemed to me as if behind the horizon of the cosmos a three-dimensional world had been artificially built up, in which each person sat by himself in a little box. ... Life and the whole world struck me as a prison, and it bothered me beyond measure that I should again be finding all that quite in order. I had been glad to shed it all, and now it had come about that I—along with everyone else—would again be hung up in a box by a thread ... everything was too material, too crude and clumsy, terribly limited spatially and spiritually. It was all an imprisonment** (Jung, 1961).

This sentiment is shared by all of us who have been through the near-death syndrome. After experiencing the limitless beauty, love, and freedom of the afterlife, coming back is a real bummer. Most people don't want to come back. Jung's description of coming back to an earthly kind of prison is right on the money.

So, why did we all come back? The answer is that during the NDE our angel guides showed every one of us that our spiritual work on earth was not complete. Everyone who has been through the experience of near death intuitively knows this to be true.

Because of the limitations and obstacles of the physical world, experiencing near death greatly heightens one's outlook on the purpose for which we are all here. The spiritual mission for all humans is to learn love and compassion—what better place than earthly existence to learn those lessons? Our being here is all part of a much bigger picture. I think Dannion Brinkley said it best:

> **these Beings were desperately trying to help us, not because we were such good guys, but because without us advancing spiritually here on earth, they could not become successful in their world ... a Being told me. "Those who go to earth are heroes and heroines, because you are doing something that no other spiritual beings have the courage to do. You have gone to earth to co-create with God"** (Brinkley, 1994).

Our every action, whether it be creative or destructive, affects the overall balance and order of the spiritual universe. It is for this reason that Hildegard maintains, "The angels are amazed by us." Hildegard further states:

> **All of the angels are amazed at humans, who through their holy works appear clothed with an incredibly beautiful garment.**

**For the angel without the work of the flesh is simply praise; but the humans with their corporeal works are a glorification** (Hildegard, 1844-91).

Because "corporeal works" or the "work of the flesh" involve risk on our part, we humans (whether we like it or not) play a key role in the "grand scheme." Free will of choice, depending on how we deal with it, can be either a burden or a joy—it is an awesome responsibility.

# 16

# BRIDGING THE GAP

***They that love beyond the world, cannot be separated. Death cannot kill what never dies. Nor can Spirits ever be divided that love and live in the same Divine Principle.***

William Penn

WHEN A HUMAN SOUL PASSES OVER into the hyper-dimension, its spiritual work doesn't come to a grinding halt. Our development as spirit beings is ongoing. In fact, our spiritual connection with the material realm remains intact. The only difference is that we are no longer bound by the physical confines and restraints imposed by space-time.

I am frequently asked, "Do the spirits of the deceased come back to us as angels?" The answer is no. Angels are not human. When human souls leave their physical bodies behind, they still have the semblance of being human.

Even in the afterlife, angels act as mediums between humans and the Divine Mind—for this reason, wherever we humans go, whether it be in this phase of life or the next, we are always in the company of angels—their guidance is always essential to our development.

It is, however, the nature of evolved human spirits to mimic their angel guides insofar as giving guidance and comfort to other human souls—this is typically manifested when the spirits of deceased relatives or friends come to help us in moments of crises. Usually this is done subtlely.

Without a doubt, at one time or another, everyone has been through the experience of sensing the presence of a deceased relative or friend trying to "get through." But there is a twofold problem: first, most of us are not in tune with the extremely high resonance through which the other dimensional communication is directed. Second, due to the effects of the mechanized "Age of Enlightenment," people generally tend to be skeptical of what they are experiencing, and dismiss such episodes of intuition as figments of their imagination—as a result, they simply are not open to receive such communication. Perhaps books such as this can help to overcome the latter part of the problem. As to the first part of the problem, communication with deceased spirits remains a matter of getting in tune with their "frequency."

Occasionally, someone with a background in physics will ask me, "What measurable range of frequency are we talking about—is it kilohertz, megahertz, gigahertz, etc?" The answer is that spiritual energy (much like light) is not a physical phenomenon. It neither behaves like particles of matter nor like electromagnetic waves—so there is no measuring it.

All of us possess the innate ability to commune with spirits of the deceased. In fact, we do this routinely in the dreamgate (this was well documented throughout the life of Edgar Cayce). Because the activity of the dreamgate takes place in the hyperdimension, dreaming automatically places our astral body on the same "wavelength" of deceased spirits. Communicating with the same spirits in the physical world, however, is a completely different matter. Remember, our physical bodies, and the material dimension in which they dwell, have density and mass, thereby resonating at extremely low frequencies; therefore, communication with the spirit world is largely a matter of bridging the gap between the two disparate levels of resonance. This is accomplished by opening oneself up, rather like a spiritual antenna, to be receptive to higher vibrations—this is called mediumship.

As the term implies, being a medium means being in the middle—acting as a kind of conduit through which spirit energy from the hyperdimension makes contact with the spiritual energy of the physical dimension.

It is not unusual, in some social settings, that someone will ask me, "Who is going to win The Superbowl," or "What are the winning lottery numbers going to be," or "Go ahead, tell me what I'm thinking." Mediums are not fortune tellers or mind readers. Contrary to the common misconception of mediums portrayed in Hollywood movies as strange, sometimes unscrupulous individuals who sit around holding hands in the dark, chanting, or talking to a Ouija board, mediums are, in fact, everyday people just like you.

Everyone is a potential medium or "sensitive." The basic element that distinguishes a person as a medium is that, at some point in the person's life, he or she has acquired or developed a unique sensitivity or receptiveness to the higher resonance of spirits. Some people are just born sensitive. Others spend years developing their receptive abilities. And some, like me, have acquired a heightened state of sensitivity through some accident or near-death experience. In some cases, mediumship is the result of several of these factors coming together.

Mediumship comes in a variety of flavors or modes of manifestation. The mediumship of mind, for example, is exactly what it denotes. It is the linking of one mind to another through transference of thought or telepathy outside the physical realm. For some mediums this is manifested as clairvoyance, "clear seeing." Through this process, mediums are able to tune in to visual impressions in their mind's eye. Typically, they will envision what the spirit looked like in its temporal life, or, the medium may even receive visions of places or objects.

Another form of telepathic communication occurs when a spirit fills the medium's mind with impressions of its emotions—this is called clairsentience, "clear feeling."

Then there is clairaudience, "clear hearing," in which the medium picks up the spirit's communication through a mental impression of its temporal voice and speech.

"Inspirational thought" is a direct transfer of pure thought. It is the same phenomenon experienced in revelatory dreaming.

When I communicate with spirits, it usually involves a combination of all the various modes of telepathy. Sometimes one mode will come through stronger than the others—in my case, this is usually due to the preference of communication on the part of the spirit. Some mediums, however, may specialize in communicating through just one particular mode.

Physical mediums are quite different from mental mediums in that they "channel" the spirit's energy through their bodies. I have yet to experience this form of spirit communication. It seems I am definitely not a channeler.

The spirits of the deceased take an active interest in our well being. They often assist our angel guides in the performance of their earthly work. In fact, it is our angel guides who quietly alert us or subtly announce to us that a spirit is desiring communication with us. Usually they do this by telepathically planting a clear and distinct thought or impression of the spirit in our minds. Most frequently, this happens at the exact moment when a relative or close friend suddenly dies—and, intuitively, *we just know.* It is the spirit's way of letting us know that they are still with us, even though they have passed from this world to the next.

People are not always receptive to the subtleties of spiritual communication. However, angel guides still know how to gently get our attention—this can involve such things as flickering lights, or household objects mysteriously tipping over, or paintings or wall ornaments suddenly lose their grip on the wall and fall to the floor, or we hear a song on the radio and it instantly compels us to think of the deceased spirit who is trying to get through to us.

Sometimes spirits will go through our highly sensitive pets to capture our attention—we see this when we notice our pet intently watching what appears to be empty space, but we sense our pet is really looking at something or someone.

Most of the communication between us and the spirit world happens because we need to learn certain spiritual lessons. There may be periods in our lives when we seem to stagnate as if our lives are not progressing—we seem to be stuck, like we're going around in circles. It's as if our every action fails to get us the results we think we want. This is a good indicator that we are not learning.

When we are unsuccessful in learning an important life lesson, it is because we are pursuing the wrong path. This pattern generally shows up as a succession of failed marriages or relationships, or as a string of unsuccessful career moves. It is not a matter of our angel guides not giving us the message, rather it is a matter of our not heeding the message. Until we learn the lesson being directed to us, our angel guides can only watch patiently as we stumble around trying to get on track, regardless of how painful the process may be. This is a critical aspect of our karmic development. If we don't learn a life lesson at a particular karmic level, we cannot advance to the next level, in this life or the next, until we learn the lesson.

Spiritual guidance doesn't mean that a spirit takes us by the hand and walks us through the maze of our life's journey. Intervening in our lives is one thing, but interfering with our learning is something that our angel guides and other loving spirits will not do—they are here to help, not hinder our development as human beings.

Our angels and other spirit guides are permitted to intervene in our lives only to the extent that we are responsive in following the correct paths we are guided to. If we are not responsive, we are not being *responsible.*

So, how do we know when we are following the right path or not? The following case history is an example of how the process works:

Janet arrived promptly at my office for her appointment. A mutual friend had recommended that she see me about a chronic problem in her life. Although she was only twenty-six years old, she had already been through two brief marriages and numerous other relationships.

She told me, "It seems I'm unlucky in love. Every relationship I have ever been in has turned out be a roller coaster ride from hell. No matter how hard I try to make things work, the men I fall in love with always end up leaving me high and dry … and miserable."

Janet was very bright and strikingly beautiful. She seemed to be the kind of lady who could have just about anything she wanted, including a good love match. But such things are not up to me to judge one way or another. I just report the communication from the other side exactly as it is given to me.

Sometimes I find it helpful to allow a client to get things out in the open rather than have them keep their thoughts and feelings pent up inside. As Janet continued, a voice suddenly filled my head. It was like an urgent phone call.

"Who is Ed?" I asked.

Janet's eyes bulged. She took a long breath. "He's my father, he passed away nearly four years ago."

"Ed is here. He wants to know if you are going to put the picture of the two of you back on the mantle?"

Janet knew exactly what I was saying. "Yes, that's a picture we took together when I was eight years old. I put it in a box right after he died. … I was angry with him. That's really weird. … I just took it out of the box the other day; I was looking at it. I'm not mad at him any more … yes, I'm going to put it back on the mantle."

Suddenly another spirit began communicating with me. It identified itself as Janet's angel guide; it filled my mind with an impression. I had to ask Janet to hold for a moment while I took it all in. I saw her father's image. He was a pleasant looking man with a tall, slender build. Then some rapid-fire scenes came through. During Janet's childhood he was drunk much of the time—she hated that. As she grew older, he was hardly ever around. And then, he vanished from her life altogether, not to be seen by her again until his funeral. Janet loved her father deeply, but she was angry with him for all the years of not being there for her.

She pursued men just like her father; they, too, were never there for her. Despite all the attempts of her angel guides to steer her in the direction of men who would be good for her, she failed to recognize them. She wasn't getting the message, and, as a result, she wasn't learning.

The angel guide brought Janet's father back into the session. Ed continued his communication with me. "Janet, your father says he is sorry for all the time he didn't spend with you. Do you understand?"

"Yes," she replied. Tears were streaming down her face.

"He also says you are going to be married again to a man who lives in a house with stained glass windows."

Janet didn't know what to make of that. She asked, "Tell me about him. ... What is he like ... how will I recognize him?"

"Your father says not to worry; when the time is right, you will know him."

Although her father's message about her marrying a man who lived in a house with stained glass didn't seem to make any sense, Janet was much relieved. Hearing from her father seemed to help clear up a lot of loose ends in her life. I saw her again the following week; she said she felt more focused and now realized that luck had nothing to do with her failed relationships.

She said, "I finally saw the light. All these years I've been looking for my father's love in men who were just like him. Each time, I was setting myself up to fail."

Janet had finally learned the lesson. Less than a year later, I heard from her again in the form of a wedding invitation. It turned out that the man she was marrying had been working in her office building for years. She had known him all along but failed to see him as a potential mate. He had a beautiful home, with stained glass windows in the front door. I reflected back to our session in my office. I remembered how Janet's father had lovingly withheld all the details about her future husband except for his stained glass windows. She still had to make the choices which led to her newfound love. The stained glass was simply an affirmation.

In bringing Janet and her father together, Janet's angel guide was able to help them both to grow spiritually. As we shall further see in the coming chapters, angel guides are always the facilitators of communication between spirits. They are the ultimate mediums of the spiritual universe.

# 17

# REAPING WHAT WE SOW

***Death is the only immortal who treats us all alike, whose pity and whose peace and whose refuge are for all— the soiled and pure, the rich and the poor, the loved and the unloved.***

Mark Twain

THROUGHOUT OUR TEMPORAL LIVES we all have to deal with an endless procession of challenges. Many of us will look upon these challenges as stumbling blocks or bad luck—instead of opportunities to learn and grow. Put simply, this is the fundamental truth of what life is all about. Our mission on earth is to learn to turn our defeats into victories—to transform life's lemons into lemonade.

Every moment in our life is an opportunity—but most of us stare opportunity in the face every day without realizing it.

Many of my clients have come to me complaining, "Life isn't fair; I never get a break." What they are really saying to me is that their lives are not fulfilled and they don't accept responsibility for it. Remember, being responsible means being responsive to the subtle, divine guidance that accompanies our every breath.

Life, in this realm and the next, is a state of mind—it is fair or unfair depending on how we assess it. If we perceive the outcome of a life challenge to be fair, then we have learned to resolve that particular issue—if we don't, the issue remains unresolved, and it will continually face us off, one way or another, until we learn to resolve it. Such unresolved issues become compounded when we see ourselves as victims of circumstances beyond our control.

A few years ago, a man and his wife came to me seeking to make contact with their teenage son who had recently died of Hodgkin's disease. Their grief was filled with anger. "How could this happen to us, why us?" Since they were not willing to resolve the issue, I hoped their son would.

The session started out with a good deal of skepticism on their part. "How will we know if Michael has really gone to heaven ... how will we know if it is really him talking to us." I assured them that if Michael wishes to make contact, he will do everything in his power to answer their questions, but it will be on his terms.

As usual, I allowed the session to proceed at its own pace. I don't keep a clock on my readings; there is no way of predicting how they will go, or how long it will take for a spirit to come through—sometimes they're just not ready. Communicating with the deceased cannot be forced.

As we sat and talked, I asked Michael's parents to focus on all of the positive aspects of his life—the good things he had done and achieved, and everything he had wished for and hoped to accomplish.

Michael didn't waste any time. He appeared to me, standing towards the rear of the couch where his parents were sitting—sort of leaning over between them with his arms folded. To expedite things, I immediately began to telepathically probe Michael's energy, asking him to give me some piece of information that only his parents would know.

"You both visited Michael's grave yesterday. He is telling me that the red carnations you placed next to his headstone was a nice touch ... you remembered that was his favorite color."

Their faces suddenly lit up like the fourth of July. "Michael is here?" they chimed.

"Yes, he's happy you came here today. He's been looking forward to this because he has a lot to tell you."

Their expressions turned sheepish, as if they were expecting Michael to bawl them out.

"Michael is showing me a silver medallion on a chain. Does that make sense to you?"

"Yes, it's his St. Christopher medal; we hung it on his headstone."

"He is also giving me the name Kim; who is Kim?"

"She is our twelve-year-old daughter. She and Michael were very close."

"He hoped you would have given his medal to her. He says he doesn't need it where he is."

"We're sorry ... we weren't thinking."

"He says that's O.K., no harm done. But he would like Kim to have his collection of rare coins ... she has always shown an interest in them." By now, Michael's parents were sobbing, the level of emotion in the room was soaring.

"Michael wants you to stop blaming yourselves for his passing; it was his death, not yours; there was nothing you could do to change it. ... He says he is happy where he is now, and he wants you to stop dwelling on what happened to him and get on with your lives."

They were almost shaking their heads in agreement. Then Michael's father made an interesting statement: "I would have done anything ... if it had been up to me, I would have gladly traded my life for his."

His father's selfless love was admirable, but Michael abruptly came back on line: "Michael is telling me that even if you could have done that, it wouldn't have solved anything ... you can't assume responsibility for what he had to go through. It was his situation to deal with, not yours. Do you understand?"

Michael's father pondered his son's revelation for a moment—I could see that it was beginning to sink in. His purpose in this world wasn't to try to live his son's life for him. At last, he understood.

"Yes," he said. "I have my hands full enough trying to live my own life."

The expression on his face revealed Michael's father to be a transformed man. He looked as though a tremendous weight had been lifted from his shoulders. I was pleased to see him now dealing with his grief in a healthy, positive way. Michael's parents thanked me and then quietly left my office.

Grief is important—it is a valuable healing process we all have to go through at various times in our lives. Shock, depression, and denial are all natural aspects of the grieving process. There is a time for all things, and there comes a time to release our grief. Carrying grief too far—"living to grieve" is counter-productive not only to our own spiritual development but to the spiritual advancement of the one we are grieving.

We truly do reap what we sow. If we sow negative energy, that is what we will reap. Positive results can only grow out of positive thoughts and actions.

# 18

# FORGIVENESS

***Forgive and act; deal with each man according to all he does, since you know his heart.***

1 Kings 8:39

***To err is human, to forgive divine.***

Alexander Pope

IT IS NOT UNUSUAL FOR DEPARTED SPIRITS and the loved ones they leave behind to have unresolved issues of guilt, and seek forgiveness from each other. Forgiveness is the great emancipator of the human spirit. Without it, we would not evolve as spiritual beings.

So, why does it take the death of a loved one to make us realize how precious that person was? And why must we first die and then go through our life review with our angel guides to feel remorse for all the rotten things we did while we were in this world? The answer is, that for all of us, death is the ultimate moment of truth. Death forces us to face ourselves—it is our final exam. Without death we would never come to grips with all of life's lessons. We've all heard the expression, "You can't cheat death," but the truer expression is, "Through death we can't cheat life."

This is where forgiveness enters the equation. It is through forgiveness that we can redeem ourselves—and then advance to a higher level of spiritual existence.

Forgiving and being forgiven is what unconditional love between humans is ultimately about—it is how we learn to love.

Remember, the laws of the spiritual universe are based on cause and effect. Sooner or later everything has to balance out. All of the selfish, cruel, unloving actions of our lives have a way of catching up with us—this translates into guilt. It is amazing how we humans go through much of our lives dragging the burden of guilt around like a boat anchor.

Guilt, like fear, is something we can run from, but we can't hide from. Most of my clients come to me seeking to ask forgiveness from a loved one who has passed on. Likewise, many of the spirits who make contact with me for the purpose of communicating with a client, seek the client's forgiveness—it is often a two-way street.

There can be, however, a unilateral, self-redeeming aspect of forgiveness through which we may offer love by simply surrendering to it.

Love is the ultimate state of mind. In her book, *A Return to Love,* Marianne Williamson lends a thoughtful insight. She says:

> **How can I forgive those who could not go past a certain wall of fear when dealing with me? How can**

> **I forgive myself for the ways in which I contributed to or participated in their fear? ... The price you pay for not taking responsibility for your own pain is the failure to realize that you can change your conditions by changing your thoughts. Regardless of who initiated a painful interaction, or how much of the error still lies in someone else's thinking, the Holy Spirit always provides you with complete escape from pain through forgiveness on your part. The other person doesn't have to consciously join you in the change** (Williamson, 1992).

In other words, somebody must bear the responsibility of making the first move—and that's a start.

Forgiveness is a manifestation of love—it is a key element to understanding the essence of God, the Divine Mind—and it translates into action from angels (or, what Williamson refers to as the Holy Spirit) which inspire us. That means that forgiveness, unlike guilt or fear, is a creative act on our part. Therefore, in order for the action of forgiveness to be complete—by that I mean a joining together by both individuals to mutually resolve their pain (or guilt)—forgiveness becomes a co-creative act in which one consciously asks for forgiveness while the other gives it.

Several years ago, a man came to me hoping to make contact with his father who had passed away four years earlier. Steve's relationship with his father had always been distant and strained. There had never been any affection between them. The usual symptoms generally associated with such a relationship, i.e., alcoholism, instability, divorce, abusive behavior, and lengthy periods of absence from each other were not factors. Steve had been a good son—his father had been a decent, responsible man, and a good family provider.

Steve said, "My dad never showed an interest in my accomplishments or achievements. I never heard any words of praise from him. I always felt like everything I did wasn't good enough or important enough in his eyes. He was not the kind of father who could be enticed into a game of 'catch,' or go see me perform in the school play. In high school, I excelled at cross-country and track. In fact, I was always the most valuable runner, and I held the distance records, not only for my school, but for the entire school league. My dad never once saw me run.

"And when I went on to college, I was an honor student, but my father didn't bother to see me graduate. It was like my dad resented me, but I have never understood why."

The love and approval he had not received from his father in life, Steve now sought in his father's death. Oddly enough, Steve seemed to want forgiveness from his father for whatever it was that he (Steve) had done wrong. Clearly this was an unresolved issue which was still eating away at him. The only way Steve's sense of unearned guilt could be resolved was to confront his father.

We began our session with a quiet prayer. I asked my angel guides for assistance in bringing Steve's father into the session. Usually, my angel guides will respond with a swift yes or no as to the spirit's desire to make contact. The response was a definite "Yes." The spirit was willing.

"Steve, I'm getting the name Mack. Is he your father?"

"Uh huh, that's him," Steve replied. "His actual name was Mackenzie, but everyone always called him Mack."

"Mack is telling me something about moving, did you recently move into a new house?"

"Yes, my wife and I just moved in two months ago."

"Well, your father says he likes it, especially the rose bushes you just planted."

"Yeah, when I was planting them, the thought crossed my mind that he would have liked them … he was always big on gardening … does he have anything else to say?"

"Mack is also giving me the name 'Vivie,' who is Vivie?"

"Vivie? … Oh, that's his nickname for my mother, Vivian … only he called her Vivie."

"O.K., but your father says the resentment he used to have towards Vivie is now gone … he is trying to communicate that to her … she always favored you over him … he hopes she can forgive him for the 'shit' he put her through."

Somehow, that seemed to strike a deep chord in Steve, I could sense his emotions rising.

True to his word, Mack had more to say.

"Mack is telling me that he is glad you are doing well; he knows he was difficult with you … he wants you to know that he always loved you, but it wasn't easy for him to show it … he's learning about being a better communicator. He's giving me an image of a man walking with a cane. Does that mean anything?"

"That has to be my grandfather, Lewis … I miss him … we always had fun together."

"Mack says he and Lewis were not close as father and son … they didn't like each other very much … wait, he is showing me a picture of you as a boy sitting on Lewis' knee, you're holding a pocket watch … your grandfather gave you lots of presents, didn't he?"

Steve chuckled, "Yes, grandpa was always good to me ... I still have that watch."

"Mack tells me he was jealous of your relationship with Lewis ... now he knows that was wrong. ... He and Lewis have patched things up ... he's asking if he can patch things up with you?"

Steve's mouth flapped wide open; he wasn't expecting that. He sat there for a moment, wearing an expression of stunned amazement.

"Yes, yes, I would like that," Steve replied.

"Mack is sorry for the pain he has caused you ... he's asking for your forgiveness ... he would like to hear you say you forgive him."

"Yes ... of course I forgive him."

I couldn't help but marvel at the incredible love I felt flow out of that moment. It was like a warm embrace. Father and son were finally united as they had never been before. They had truly bridged the gap between this world and the next—and bridged the gap between guilt and forgiveness.

# 19

# LOST SOULS

***Self is the only prison that can ever bind the soul.***

Henry Van Dyke

## Prisoners of the Ego

NOT ALL SOULS who take permanent leave of their physical bodies succeed in making a smooth transition from this world to the next. The reason for this is that sometimes, when a person's earthly life comes to a sudden and violent end, his or her spirit is not aware that it has died. On this, Emanuel Swedenborg wrote:

> **A certain spirit came to me not long after his decease, which I was able to conclude from this circumstance, that as yet he knew not that he was in the other life, imagining that he still lived in the world. ... I discoursed with him; but then suddenly he was taken up on high, which surprised me. ... Presently, however, I perceived that he was taken up amongst the angelic spirits. ... From this situation**

> **he afterwards discoursed with me, saying, that he saw things of such sublimity as no human comprehension could conceive** (Swedenborg, 1854).

Believing itself to be in the dreamgate, the confused spirit remains in the physical plane occupying familiar places with which it is emotionally attached. These disoriented spirits are lost, or "dispossessed" souls.

Lost souls, or "ghosts," not only remain attached to the physical world, they are also attached to what Eastern religions call *ego consciousness*—they have shed their physical bodies but not their egos.

Ego consciousness is the selfish "I, me, my syndrome." It is our ego which acts as an illusionary barrier that keeps us from realizing the divinity within us.

A spirit that won't let go of its ego is devolved—rather than advancing to a higher level of spiritual development, it declines to a much lower level. Such spirits are thought to be "evil" or "demonic," however, such terms are misused.

Lost souls are not evil, they are unenlightened—they fail to distinguish the illusory aspects of space-time from the illusion of ego consciousness. Thus, they cling to a seemingly endless cycle of self-deception.

I know this sounds spooky, but because lost souls dwell in a murky, negative level of existence; they tend to generate a dark field of negative energy around them. This dark field can actually be psychically observed through clairvoyance—it appears like a shroud around the "ghost" as a dark, vaporous veil or black mist. I have personally witnessed this phenomenon on several occasions, and, I must say, it's a very eerie experience.

It is because of this dark mist of negative energy that lost souls have difficulty leaving the physical plane—ego consciousness thrives here. But the negative energy is the spirit's own creation—it is the lowest state of being.

So long as the bewildered spirit ambles around, tripping over its own negative thoughts, it is, in a sense, doomed. As we shall see further in Chapter 20, "Their Thoughts" keep them prisoners of "This Little World."

The lost soul must first release itself from its ego consciousness and all of the restraints of space-time before it can free itself from the physical realm. The spirit's angel guides are not permitted to interfere with its karmic progress; they can only serve as guides not rescuers; therefore, they can only wait until the lost soul finally finds its way out, and emerges from the dark mist into their loving glow.

The motion picture, *The Exorcist,* gave us a totally, inaccurate, sensationalized picture of what it is like to encounter such spirits. The encounter may be a harrowing experience, but it does not involve "possession" by the dispossessed spirit—not even for channelers.

Sometimes, those of us living in the earthly realm are able to help the lost soul find its way into the spiritual realm where it belongs. There have been times in my life when I have been involved with such ventures.

Late one night, about nine years ago, I received an urgent phone call from a client. His sister's boyfriend had recently been killed in a gruesome motorcycle accident. Not only was she grieving his loss, but she had begun to experience strange anomalies in her apartment.

Most of these occurrences were happening late at night into the early hours of the morning. Water would suddenly spew out of the kitchen and bathroom faucets. The stereo would erupt with blaring music, startling her out of a sound sleep.

With each passing day, the situation grew progressively worse. Puddles of water were mysteriously appearing in the middle of the living room floor. Her alarm clock began to go off every night at 1:52 am—the exact time Keith had come to his untimely death.

Then, one evening, as she stepped out of the shower, Sharon found an inscription scrawled, as if by an invisible finger, on her steamed, bathroom mirror. It read:

**KEITH**
**AND**
**SHARON**
**FOREVER!**

That was it. Sharon knew Keith was there with her. In life, he liked to surprise her by leaving love doodles on that same mirror. But Sharon was at her wits end. "I will always love Keith, but it's fucking, freaking me out," she said. This unnatural routine, perpetrated by Keith's restless spirit, had to stop.

I met Sharon at her apartment the next day. I explained some of the details we would go through in "cleansing" her apartment. But most important was the matter of confronting Keith's spirit. I lit some sage, and said a prayer, invoking my angel guides.

Hobbs appeared, which is not unusual. Our guardian angels are always directly involved whenever we are confronted by negative, spiritual energy.

Hobbs said, "If you choose to confront this spirit, do not give into its fear or yours. Its negative energy feeds on fear. Think and feel only the love and compassion that is within you."

A cold chill slipped over me like an icy hand. I could sense the presence of Keith's spirit in the room. I instructed Sharon to open the window blinds and curtains to allow as much sunlight into the room as possible.

A faint, shadowy form sought refuge from the corner of my eye as I looked over at an area of the room most sheltered from the sun's direct rays.

The diffused image of Keith's spirit was further obscured by a dark, cascading vapor which appeared to dissolve into a watery substance dripping down the lower portion of the wall—it was like an impenetrable barrier separating our thoughts.

The negative vibes were practically overwhelming, but Hobbs' instructions filled me to capacity—I could only feel divine love—there is truly no force more powerful than that.

I felt my energy gradually pierce through the dark shroud which was holding Keith's spirit prisoner in the physical plane. At last, we were able to communicate.

I asked, "Do you know where you are?"

Keith responded, "I'm not sure. ... I don't understand what's happening to me."

I probed further. "Do you remember your motorcycle accident?"

"No ... what motorcycle accident?"

"Think back. It was late at night, you were riding your bike, you were pissed off at something that had happened earlier. Do you remember that?"

"Yeah, Sharon and I had gotten into a big fight over something ... I don't remember what ... I just remember jumping on my bike and getting the hell out."

"O.K., hold that thought. As you were riding, do you remember a big, blue van running a stop light, plunging right into you?"

"No, I never saw a van. ... Are you telling me I'm dead?"

"Yes, you died. You are no longer in your physical body, do you understand?"

There was a deafening silence. Then I saw a flash of brilliant light. An angel guide appeared as if summoning Keith to go with it. The black mist, like Keith's ghost, had somehow evaporated into thin air.

In that instant, Keith, and Sharon, had truly found peace.

# PART FOUR

# SYNTHESIS

# 20

# THE HOUSE OF SPIRITS
## *Signposts to the Hyperdimension*

***I don't think we're in Kansas anymore, Toto!***

Dorothy, *The Wizard of Oz*

***It gets curiouser and curiouser!***

Alice, *Through The Looking Glass*
by Lewis Carroll

HERETOFORE, IT HAS BEEN MY INTENTION to guide the reader through an introspective and, hopefully, enlightening odyssey. Throughout the pages of the preceding chapters, the reader has been provided with an intrinsic look into a variety of different phenomena—which, by themselves, appear to be diverse aspects of all existence. Like quantum particles, or modes of resonance, no single aspect is more significant than the other. I trust that you, the reader, have *always known,* intuitively, that all things, at *the highest level,* become *ONE*—be it *Angels, Out-of-Body Experience, Near-Death Experience, Communicating with the Deceased,* the *Dreamgate,* the *Hyperdimension,* or what the philosopher Rudolph Otto referred to as *Numinous Consciousness,* or what Pierre Teilhard de Chardin called *The Omega Point* (more on this later).

We have now arrived at the apex, *the point* where ALL other points merge together in a higher SYNTHESIS. If the reader is ready and willing, we will now enter the realm of what lies beyond *space-time-matter,* and *Death.* But remember, this is still an odyssey.

She has always been with me! For most of my earthly life I didn't recognize or understand "who she was" or "why she was." She is awesome—a spirit to be reckoned with! And she has a message totally beyond description—it is a powerful message from beyond her grave, and it was conceived twenty-four years before I was born. Fifty-two years later, through the intuitive process called *Inspirational Thought,* she started to communicate directly with me—only after I began the writing of this book!

The reader should also know that she is the embodiment, the essence of what this book is ultimately about. It is about the psychic bridge between spiritual and material existence—which can only be reached by achieving the self-revealing mastery of our higher, intuitive faculties. In this regard, she is the paradigm of this book. Every word, every sentence, every thought—leads us to her and through her—a brilliant portal from this world to the next.

## The Lady and Her Mystery—and the Way She Reveals It

In the spring of 1998 I toured one of the most unique and mysterious homes ever built—the house, in fact, is a California Historical Landmark. As might be expected, it is grand in size, 160 rooms, encompassing four acres.

Blending in with the rest of the tourists, I wandered through the vast maze of strangely constructed rooms with upside-down columns, and stairs and chimneys which come to an abrupt halt just inches from their ceilings—and doors that, when opened, reveal solid walls instead of passage to some other room or space. Some rooms have skylights above skylights, while other rooms have skylights covered with roofs, and, in at least one case, a skylight fashioned into the floor. To make matters more intriguing, the house is replete with the redundant appearance of the mystical numbers 7, 11, and 13 manifested in its architectural design and fixtures. The oddities of the house are endless.

Was this strange architecture a silly joke, or was there some abstruse meaning or purpose built into its scheme? In many respects, I saw parallels between the house's conceptual design and the ideas embedded in the works of M.C. Escher. It was clear to me that a higher dimensional perspective had been purposefully incorporated into the construction of the house. The architect and resident of this exquisite "Mystery Mansion" had been Sarah Pardee Winchester, heiress to the fabulous Winchester rifle fortune.

I was well aware of the amazing history of the house and its late owner. I was further cognizant of the existing theories and rumors about Sarah Winchester having been an eccentric, crazy spiritualist who had built the house for the edification and appeasement of "angry spirits" who had all been killed by Winchester firearms. But, I knew there was far more to the story than people realized.

She was born Sarah L. Pardee in 1840. The daughter of a high-society couple in New Haven, Connecticut, Sarah was beautiful, charming, and highly intelligent. By the time she reached debutante age, young Sarah was an accomplished musician, a voracious reader of all forms of literature, and a master of four languages. Despite her diminutive size (4'10") she was widely regarded as "The Belle of New Haven."

In 1862, Sarah married William Wirt Winchester, son of Oliver Fisher Winchester, who was the founder of the Winchester Repeating Arms Company. Contrary to popular sentiment, her attraction ran far deeper than William's wallet. For reasons that will be made clear later in this chapter, Sarah regarded William as her perfect soul mate. Four years later, Sarah gave birth to a baby girl. Little Annie, was totally blanketed in her mother's adoring love. Sarah held high aspirations for her, not only because Annie was her daughter, but she was also esteemed by her mother as a spiritual twin. As fate would have it, Annie Winchester died forty days after her birth. Sarah would never get over the devastating loss.

The grieving years that followed Annie's death were further compounded by her father's slow, deteriorating demise due to a losing battle with tuberculosis. The double loss of her daughter and husband seemed like a curse, but Sarah Winchester was not one to give up on life.

Although she was now heiress to the Winchester rifle fortune, worth twenty million dollars plus royalties, the widow Winchester sought solace not in worldly affairs, but rather in the spiritual domain.

The new tide of philosophical thinking which, in the coming years, would influence the likes of Einstein and Escher (and Sarah Winchester) was already sweeping through the European and North American continents. Centuries of European colonialism in the East had created a fusion of oriental and occidental spiritualism. Buddhist and Hindu concepts about the afterlife, astral projection, and telepathy, conjoined with ancient Pythagorean and Kabbalistic mysticism (particularly their emphasis on the secret ciphering of numbers), were seeping through the cracks of Christian traditionalism.

Secret societies, such as the Kabbalists, Rosicrucians, and Freemasons, were mingling with one another, producing a synthesis of "esoteric mysticism" which was well ahead of its time.

The latter part of the nineteenth century saw a widespread interest among European and American intellectuals in the esoteric writings of Albertus Magnus, Paracelsus, Emanuel Swedenborg, Madame Helena Blavatsky, and Rudolf Steiner—such writers laid the foundation of a new spiritual philosophy called *Theosophy* which Sarah Winchester embraced wholeheartedly.

A medium in her own right, Sarah traveled abroad to confer with the leading spiritualists, mediums, swamis, and yogis of Europe and India. It seems she selectively adopted certain elements of various spiritual doctrines into her own—albeit, Theosophy, without a doubt, remained the primary spiritual influence throughout the remainder of Mrs. Winchester's life.

However, since Sarah neglected to write about her personal, spiritual views, how are we to know them? The answer is that her spiritualism is indelibly etched in the construction of her home.

Sarah was certainly impressed with the secrecy inherent in the esoteric philosophies which had influenced her. She loved a good mystery! In fact, writing and participating in mystery plays was one of the "preliminary disciplines" espoused by the Theosophist writer, Rudolf Steiner—such activity would lead one to "higher levels of insight." As we shall see, Mrs. Winchester took meticulous care in writing the mystery of her life and her spiritualism in every aspect of her home. She had a message and a mission.

In 1884 Sarah Winchester moved from the east coast to California's Santa Clara Valley whereupon she took up residence in an eighteen-room farm house. The rumormongers have always maintained she settled there because the area had a scarcity of thunderstorms—it was erroneously believed that her daughter had died in a fire caused by lightning.

Sarah immediately hired a staff of carpenters and began construction of her Mystery House. The construction and the incessant sound of pounding hammers would go on twenty-four hours a day, 365 days a year for nearly four decades, stopping only upon Sarah's death in 1922. One of the most prominent rumors attempting to explain Sarah's obsession with the never-ending construction suggests she was motivated by a spirit medium who had informed her that the Winchester fortune was cursed as a result of all those who had died (mostly Native Americans) at the mercy of a weapon made by Winchester. Moreover, as the rumor goes, the medium instructed Sarah that the spirits demanded she build them a house that would never cease to grow. Any stop or delay of the construction would bring about her instant demise. The great flaw in this rumor lies in the fact that Sarah, being an enlightened spiritualist, had no justifiable fear of passing on into the afterlife.

So, what then was the real purpose for the nonstop construction? The answer is to be found in Sarah's Theosophical thinking. Theosophy teaches a monistic view of the universe as a vast, living organism (not a mechanism) in which all living beings are likened to individually evolving entities or cells that comprise a greater universal body. Such a universe is "EVER BUILDING" in that each individual spirit is an integral, synergistic part of the entire, universal, organic process. One grows and evolves to higher levels of universal consciousness through intuitive thinking—this involves exercising and building one's higher faculties, and the pursuit of higher, individual revelation. Those who prove themselves worthy of the supreme knowledge of divinity may gain access to the ultimate spiritual reality which transcends material existence (this is quite similar to Carl Jung's concept of "The Collective Unconscious" and Pierre Teilhard de Chardin's "Omega Point"). An individual's spiritual growth and development can be manifested through thought and art (which can include architecture).

Sarah is reputed to have made the statement, "a house that does not grow rots," just as a body that does not grow rots—she clearly saw the House as a living organism which was both a manifestation of her spiritual growth and a literal extension of her physical body.

One of the most common misconceptions about unlocking the secrets of Sarah's mystery house is that the key lies hidden in the seance room. After all, it was her most secretive room. Until her death, Sarah was the only earthly soul to have access to it. To this day, many people, including the likes of Harry Houdini, have looked to the seance room to reveal the secrets of Sarah's mystery. I'm reminded of a line from *Indiana Jones*, "They're digging in the wrong place." Sarah, in fact, laid it all out in plain view ... in the Ballroom. Ahh yes, there is a catch—you still have to figure out the "key."

Actually, there are three basic keys to unlocking the mystery of Sarah's thoughts. Each key (conceptually) is linked with the other two. The mystery cannot be solved without the synergistic application of all three keys—this requires the use of intuition and insight.

The first key lies in unlocking the mystery of the two stained-glass window panes which flank both sides of the fireplace in the House's Ballroom. Each glass pane bears a separate, cryptic inscription from Shakespeare. The inscription on the first window pane (left of the fireplace) reads:

*WIDE. UNCLASP.*
*THE. TABLES. OF.*
*THEIR. THOUGHTS.*

The inscription on the second window pane (on the right side of the fireplace) reads:

**Shakespearean Windows**

Courtesy of The Winchester Mystery House

*THESE. SAME.*
*THOUGHTS. PEOPLE.*
*THIS. LITTLE. WORLD.*

The initial response most people have when reading these lines is that the words, in each inscription, seem to be misplaced or out of order. As sentences, they have an unfinished, incomplete quality to them—that is precisely what motivated Sarah to display them. She intentionally wants the reader of the inscriptions to be drawn in to ponder the mystery of their meaning. Thus, the two window panes bearing the cryptic phrases are both a carefully crafted puzzle and signpost, and were deliberately mounted into their respective places on the Ballroom wall to entice and perplex the initiate observer.

Sarah's use of these particular Shakespearean phrases also bears witness to her monumental eruditeness. She had to have known Shakespeare's voluminous works inside out and backwards in order to extract these specific lines the way she did. As any Shakespearean scholar knows, it is extremely rare to find such seemingly jumbled lines in the man's work.

Was Sarah merely taunting the observer with her intellectual prowess, or was she in pursuit of a much loftier purpose? The answer is the latter. One of her prime motives for incorporating such detailed mystery and wonder in her "art" is that she seeks to enlighten us! Not only does she invite us to unlock her mystery, but, in the process, she wants to exhort us to a path of self-revelation. Remember, from Sarah's Theosophical point of view, we, as individuals, must be compelled to use our higher faculties of insight in order to achieve higher levels of consciousness. In a sense, she is inducing us to reach toward a heavenly consciousness.

So, what are we to see in the inscriptions? The first line seems to coax the readers to open up (unclasp) their minds. The second line, in conjunction with the first, seems to suggest that if we (people) free our thoughts from the small confines of worldly existence, we may be able to climb to a consciousness which transcends our (little) world. Such intuitive exercise could be likened to walking up flights of stairs to gain a higher perspective—as we shall see, Sarah symbolically applies "these same thoughts" to her design of the numerous flights of stairs throughout the House.

As we continue our ascent up the stairs of our intuition we find ourselves bumping into sudden bursts of insight which lead us to an ever higher and widening point of view—this is precisely what happens when we unlock the door to each progressive flight of intuitive stairs. Now go back and look at the inscriptions. Can you see more meaning in them? Are you beginning to see things more clearly through your "ethereal" eyes?

Most people who have taken up the quest to decipher the message hidden in the two window panes try to expand the meaning of the words themselves by rearranging them like an anagram. But such attempts only take the observer further away from unlocking the mystery. Remember, when Sarah extracted these lines from Shakespeare she took them exactly in the *order* that Shakespeare wrote them, so that we would be awakened by their apparent *disorder*.

The problem people invariably run into when trying to "crack the code" is that they persist in using their powers of rigid rationale, rather than yielding to their higher powers of intuition (this process, by the way, is what Einstein claimed to have always led him to his sudden bursts of insight). Sarah deliberately devised the mystery so that we may be enlightened only if we choose the path to higher insight. This brings us to the second key.

If our intuitive stair-climbing has led us to realize the first insight, we will now be able to see that there are words beyond the words we observe in the inscriptions. But where are these words? Why don't we see them? The answer lies in finding them from a higher dimensional point of view.

Sarah was well aware of higher dimensions—this is aptly demonstrated in her construction of the stairs that lead up to the ceiling, and the doors that open onto solid walls. Ludicrous rumors have always tried to explain such anomalous features as being devices to confuse evil spirits. The truth is, from her higher dimensional perspective, Sarah could envision the stairs and the doors leading into the hyperdimension.

Thus it is, with regard to the Shakespearean glass windows. Shakespeare's words are artfully depicted as being inscribed on a ribbon or banner that winds round and round in a corkscrew fashion. Unless the observer surveys the glass panes from a higher dimensional point of view, he or she will only see some artistically, painted words with aesthetic lines and geometric patterns around them on a flat, two-dimensional surface. If we could see the banner, on which the observed words are written, three dimensionally, we could then perceive that there must be more words that cannot be observed on the other side of its twisted surface. However, once we conceive of taking our perception of the banner up to a higher level of dimension (beyond three dimensions) we would then have the ability to observe the words written on the banner's other side—this is the second insight Sarah hoped the observer would arrive at. Furthermore, she wanted the observer to come to the realization that higher dimensions are not spatial, but are dimensions of Mind.

It should then come as no surprise to the enlightened observer, that Sarah didn't bother to have the rest of the Shakespearean text painted on the backside of the windows. She knew that once the observer reached the second insight, he or she would simply consult the Shakespearean plays from which the two lines had been taken—with the understanding that it would lead to a wellspring of knowledge she wanted the observer to discover.

The two Shakespearean texts in question are Act IV, scene V of *Troilus and Cressida*, and Act V, scene V of *Richard II*. Notice the chronological sequence of the two scenes. This is no accident. As we shall see, Sarah took great care to weave synchronicity into the fabric of her multifaceted mystery—always with a higher purpose in mind.

The two scenes represent two different sides of Sarah's personality, her feminine side (in *Troilus and Cressida*) and her masculine side (in *Richard II*). They also represent two disparate phases in her life, an early (young) phase, and a later (mature) phase.

With regard to the first scene, Sarah's youthful, feminine side identifies with Cressida. Like Cressida, young Sarah Winchester's beauty was matched, equally, by her sharp, discerning wit. As New Haven's leading debutante, she had mastered all of the coquettish skills that young women in high society are compelled to learn, and she was quite familiar with the jagged, edged, social environment governed by

***sluttish spoils of opportunity,***
***And daughters of the game.***

Like Cressida, Sarah is a SURVIVOR—a salient point she wants the observer to recognize.

Another revealing feature of this scene which Sarah trusted the observer to find is in the structural metaphor Shakespeare uses in giving us a physical and spiritual description of Cressida. For example:

***There's language in her eye, her cheek, her lip,***
***At every joint and motive of her body.***
***O, these encounters, so glib of tongue,***
***That give a coasting welcome ere it comes,***
***And wide unclasp the tables of their thoughts***
***To every ticklish reader!***

Sarah wanted the observer to see the relationship of the metaphor with the line inscribed on the glass window pane. Shakespeare describes Cressida as though she is an artistic work in progress. It is here that Sarah seeks to educe from us a much deeper understanding of her. Not only does she see Cressida as a younger version of herself, she also sees her as a model of what her daughter Annie would have been like had she SURVIVED—as we shall further see, Sarah left very specific clues to substantiate this fact. Moreover, Sarah views *her artistic work* in progress (the House) as both an extension and embodiment of her own spirit along with William's spirit and Annie's spirit. The House is an earthly, microcosmic representation of the Theosophical view of the universal body—it is not simply a structure made of wood and brick; it is a living, growing organism whose spirit is a higher synthesis of Sarah, William, and Annie.

It is important to note that the second phase of Sarah's life takes place after the great San Francisco earthquake of 1906. The damage to the house was quite extensive. Prior to the earthquake, the house had reached seven stories in some places, but the cataclysm had caused the top three stories to come tumbling down. They were never rebuilt.

The scene from *Richard II*, from which the second Shakespearean inscription is to be found, shows us an older, more cynical Sarah Winchester. Here, she identifies with a vanquished, imprisoned, cynical Richard:

> ***I have been studying how I may compare***
> ***This prison where I live unto the world:***
> ***And, for because the world is populous,***
> ***And here is not a creature but myself,***
> ***I cannot do it;—yet I'll hammer't out.***

Through these lines, Sarah likens herself to a prisoner of the earthly world. Because she sees the world from a much different perspective than other people, she finds herself all alone—with the exception of the House. It is her only purpose for existing on the earthly plane. She seems to ponder whether or not her purpose is futile. But she answers her own question in the resolute statement, "yet I'll hammer't out." For Shakespeare, this is meant figuratively, but for Sarah, *hammering it out* has a more literal meaning. Remember, the House is the living, synergistic, embodiment of Sarah, William, and Annie on earth. However, the synthesis of their three spirits, in one, higher, greater spirit, transcends the material dimension as an integral part of the Divine Mind.

Through the line inscribed on the second window pane, we are directed to the rest of the lines which encompass it. Here, Sarah concludes her case for the *synthesis* as the House now speaks to us:

***My brain I'll make the female to my soul,***
***My soul the father: and these two beget***
***A generation of still-breeding thoughts,***
***And these same thoughts people this little world,***
***In humors like the people of this world,***
***For no thought is contented. The better sort,—***
***As thoughts of things divine,—are intermix'd***

The third key to unlocking the mystery is intertwined with the other two. Again, Sarah's Theosophical thinking comes into the overall equation. As with the esoteric, spiritual traditions of the Kabbalists, Pythagoreans, and Platonists, Theosophy is intricately connected to the divinity in numbers—known as *numerology*.

Contrary to what some people may think, numerology is neither a mystical toy nor a device for playing tricks with numbers. Numbers are not invented. They literally have a life of their own, and their relationship to all things spiritual or material, exist as an independent reality.

Although numerology does not determine our destinies, it does reveal them—it is the product of the dynamic symmetry inherent in the divine perfection of numbers—transcendent of space-time constraints. Mathematics is a construct of pure thought. Einstein said "the creative principle resides in mathematics. In a certain sense, therefore, I hold it true that pure thought can grasp reality, as the ancients dreamed."

Physicists and mathematicians are at a loss to explain how and why numerology works. They do, however, acknowledge that "some kind of deep numerology is woven into the symmetrical structure of the universe." Moreover, numerological relationships are clearly a construct of higher dimensions. In essence, numerology IS higher dimensional mathematics.

Sarah uses numerology to help us validate our insights and to show us how she, William, and Annie are intricately connected in their higher "Synthesis."

For the most part, Sarah adheres to the traditional "modern numerology." As we shall see, however, there are specific situations in which she applies her own higher dimensional brand of numerology in order to inform and enlighten us.

Modern numerology is really quite simple. It assigns three numbers to any given name. One number is applied to the vowels, another goes with the consonants, culminating in a third, ruling number which is the sum of the other two. In the case of birth dates, all of the birth numbers are simply added together resulting in one simplified number.

The numbers 1 through 9 are used in the calculation, and they are assigned to the letters of the alphabet as follows:

| 1 | 2 | 3 | 4 | 5 | 6 | 7 | 8 | 9 |
|---|---|---|---|---|---|---|---|---|
| A | B | C | D | E | F | G | H | I |
| J | K | L | M | N | O | P | Q | R |
| S | T | U | V | W | X | Y | Z | |

Now simply add the vowels in a name, then add up its consonants, and then add the sum of the vowels to the sum of the consonants and you will arrive at a simplified, ruling number. Thus, in adding up the numbers for Christopher Scott, we get 81 which, added together, would give me the numerological number 9.

All numerological expressions possess different spiritual attributes which reveal much about a person's character and destiny. For example, a person whose number is 9 tends to be people oriented. Nines have a natural need to help others. They are nurturing and understanding, and have strong, humanitarian values and interests.

There are two additional numbers, beyond the basic 1 through 9, which are considered to possess the highest qualities of spiritual enlightenment. These are the "master" numbers 11 and 22. Eleven is the number of intuition, insight, and revelation. People who are elevens have a powerful, visionary message which must be shared with the rest of the world. People who are endowed with the numerological number twenty-two are the spiritual masters—they are the sages of the world. The master number 11 can be simplified to 2 (1+1) and vice versa. Likewise, 22 can be expressed more simply as 4 (2+2), or, 4 can be expressed more highly as 22.

Sarah seemed to focus on the numerology inherent in names. While making use of standard numerology, she succeeded in developing a more evolved numerology in which certain numbers can be seen to be more intricately connected.

Sarah applied her numerology, for example, to her maiden name Sarah Pardee. Conventionally, the name Sarah would equal the number 20, and the name Pardee equals 31. The sum of the two numbers then comes to 51, then 5+1= 6. But that's not how she saw it. First, the number 20 becomes 2, while the number 31 becomes 4. Instead of adding 2 and 4 together, she left them separate (expressed as 24). Then, 2 rotates into 11, and 4 rotates into 22 (much the way that space and time rotate into each other).

Sarah possesses both of the master numbers. Moreover, the conjugation of 2 (Sarah) and 4 (Pardee) in the number 24 serves as the *foundation* of her higher dimensional numerology. Furthermore, the numbers 2 and 4 simplify to 8 through multiplication: 2x4= 8 which then rotates into 44—as we shall see, this is all critical in Sarah's numerology.

Sarah Pardee basically saw her numerological number to be eleven; notice the sum of the letters in the first and last names count out to eleven.

When she met William, she found his numbers to be 7, 7, and 7 (i.e., William = 34 =7, Wirt = 25 =7, and Winchester = 52 = 7. In modern numerology, seven is considered to be the "perfect number," the number of eternity and completion—consistent with the supreme level of spiritual consciousness (or, what I refer to as "Omega Consciousness").

Rather than add the three sets of the number 7 (or its rotations) together, Sarah applied the same higher dimensional approach to William's numerology as she did her own by keeping the numbers separate, expressed, comprehensively, as 777. In fact, she affirmed her view of William's numerology by maintaining exactly 777 shares of stock in the Winchester Repeating Arms Company throughout the years following William's untimely death.

Furthermore, Sarah's higher dimensional numerology, as it applied to William, resulted in an uncanny symmetry and unification of her own numbers by simply multiplying the number 7 exponentially, so that 7x7= 49 which then simplifies to 13. 49x49= 2,401—the sum of this number is 7. Another way to approach the equation is to add 4+9= 13. Then 13 multiplied by itself equals 169= 16= 7. As we shall see, this is important stuff.

When Sarah married William, she became Sarah Pardee Winchester. Using conventional numerology, her name was now equivalent to 13. For Sarah, the number thirteen became the most important number because it represents a higher synthesis of the numbers 7 and 11. Notice the difference between the two numbers is 4 which then rotates into its higher expression of 13. Moreover, as we have seen, 4 also rotates into the master number 22. So, from Sarah's higher dimensional perspective, 13 and 22 rotate into each other—now multiply them together, and we get 286, the sum of which is 16 which, then, transforms into 7. Remember, all things become simplified when expressed from a higher dimensional point of view. Now multiply 13x13, or, 22x22, in either case, we still get a numerological 7. The name Sarah Pardee Winchester adds up to a numerological 103, William Wirt Winchester equals 111, when added together, their numbers become 214 which then equals 7.

Annie's numerology bears out both the numbers 7 and 11. Annie Winchester = 77. As we've seen, 7 multiplied by itself, exponentially, will still render a 7. And if we multiply 7x11 we still get the same outcome twice over.

When Annie died, her obituary in a New Haven newspaper read: "Winchester, in this city, July 24, 1866,

ANNIE PARDEE, infant daughter of William Wirt and Sarah L. Winchester." Notice how the name Annie Pardee is stressed, and, in reference to Sarah, the name Pardee is replaced by her maiden, middle initial L. Sarah most certainly wanted the obituary to read this way—it demonstrated her intense feeling of spiritual kinship with her daughter. The name Annie Pardee numerologically equals 56 which then equals 11. Moreover, her actual birth name, Anne, coupled with Pardee equals 47 which also equals 11. However, Sarah preferred the name Annie Pardee because (as with the name Sarah Pardee) when we count out all of the letters in the first and last names, we still get 11.

The numbers 7, 11, and 13 share another important attribute—they are all *prime numbers*. Prime numbers are divisible only by themselves and the number 1. This is consistent with the Theosophical *monistic* view of existence.

As we shall further see, the symmetrical, higher dimensional rotation of the numbers 7, 11, and 13 is the critical ingredient to understanding their monistic relationship.

The vast majority of people who go through the Winchester House, observing the overwhelming redundancy of the mystical numbers in its structure, have no idea that they are staring the numerological billboards directly in the face. They invariably believe seven and eleven to be nothing more than lucky numbers, and the superfluous appearance of the number thirteen to be an ominous talisman aimed at warding off bad spooks.

Sarah, however, provided the observer some subtle clues designed to reveal the numerological, third key to unlocking her mystery. The Ballroom of the House has nine ceiling panels (or, more precisely, 1 through 9 panels), each having thirteen sub panels. This is an important clue. Sarah wants the observer to realize the importance of both numbers, and their respective connections to unlocking the mystery.

Assuming the enlightened observer may have some knowledge or awareness of numerology, it should not then require a quantum leap of understanding to recognize the number nine (or numbers 1 through 9) to be a signpost directing the observer to extrapolate thirteen as a number of utmost numerological significance. And, even if the intuitive observer remains clueless, the number nine, openly displayed in the Ballroom's ceiling, still serves as a subtle road map that entices the observer to comprehend that there must be some revelatory connection between numbers nine and thirteen—more consummately, the observer might gain the insight of the numerological (1 through 9) unification of the numbers 7, 11, and 13.

Sarah, in fact, knew that once the observer understood the basic dynamics of her higher dimensional numerology, it would then lead to the simple multiplication of 9x13 which equals 117. But it's not 117 that Sarah wants the observer to see, rather it is the juxtaposition of the numbers 11 and 7. Thus, 11 (Sarah) stands hand-in-hand with 7 (William). Of course, it doesn't stop there. Sarah wants the observer to go further by multiplying 11x7, the product of which is 77 which then equals Annie Winchester.

Although the panels in the Ballroom ceiling serve as a prominent and obvious device to induce us into realizing that numerology is imperative to unlocking the mystery, Sarah literally took steps to further enlighten us. Towards the rear of the House, we find its most outrageous flight of stairs known as the "switchback" staircase—it has 44 tiny steps with 7 turns. Each step is approximately 2 inches in height. This is no accident. As with other anomalies throughout the House, Sarah wanted the observer to be drawn-in to ponder the meaning of these strange steps with their redundant zig-zag pattern.

The switchback staircase, in fact, functions as a sort of primer through which Sarah reveals how her higher dimensional brand of numerology works. First, she wants the observer to look at the numbers 44 and 7. Second, she wants us to see that the stairs rise only to a height of 9 feet.

Knowing the significance of the number nine, the enlightened observer is compelled to deal with the numbers 44 and 7 numerologically. Sarah knew that we would begin by adding 44 and 7, thus arriving at 51. She also knew this would lead us to her maiden name, i.e., 51 equals Sarah Pardee.

But why Pardee rather than Winchester? Like the Shakespearean verses, she wants the observer to realize that stopping here leaves things incomplete. Something is missing; she wants us to go further. Because we know the name Sarah Pardee is numerologically equivalent to 51, we also know that Winchester is equivalent to 52. This is no coincidence. As with the juxtaposed relationship between the numbers 11 (Sarah) and 7 (William), Sarah wants us to see the synchronous relationship of the numbers 51 (Sarah Pardee) and 52 (Winchester).

Next, Sarah wants the observer to add 51 and 52, thus arriving at 103 (Sarah Pardee Winchester) which then simplifies to 13. We have now gained a minor insight that the significance of the number 13 involves numerologically merging Sarah's maiden name with her married name. In other words, William and Sarah's numerologies reveal a common destiny between them.

But what of the numbers? We see the name Winchester embodied in the number 7. How does the number 11 fit the equation?

We remember that unraveling the meaning behind the Shakespearean inscriptions demanded a higher dimensional approach. Sarah wants the observer to apply "These Same Thoughts" by now multiplying 44x7 which then results in 308 simplifying to 11. Now the pattern of Sarah's higher dimensional numerology begins to emerge.

Armed with new insight, we return to the name Sarah Pardee. We remember the importance of rotating the numbers, in order to arrive at their higher dimensional expressions. Prior to her marriage, Sarah Pardee saw her first name (numerologically expressed as 20) simplified as 2 which then realizes its highest expression when rotated into the master number 11. Similarly, the name Pardee (expressed numerologically as 31) simplifies to 4 which then rotates into the master number 22.

However, 22, unlike 11, is not a prime number; thus, for Sarah, 22 couldn't be the highest expression of 4. Therefore, since 4 and 22 are not prime numbers, their highest expression is realized only when they rotate into the prime number 13. But the significance of 13 could not be manifested until William came into the picture—and, as we shall further see, the numerologies of the prominent New Haven couple were already intertwined long before they ever met. When Sarah married William, 13 became the *perfect, higher unification* of Sarah (11) and William (7).

We return to the number 44. Sarah most certainly didn't introduce the number into the equation by random chance. It must have meaning. Since 7 represents the simplified expression of the name Winchester, is it possible that 44 somehow engenders a higher dimensional approach to the name Sarah Pardee? The answer is yes. As we have seen, the name Sarah equals 20, and Pardee equals 31. When simplified, the 20 equals 2 while the 31 equals 4, resulting in a juxtaposition of 2 and 4 (expressed as the number 24). We have also seen how 2 rotates into 11, and 4 rotates into 22 and 13.

Instead of adding these numbers, Sarah's higher dimensional methodology (as we have seen) involves multiplication. So, when we multiply 2x4 we get **8** which then rotates into 44, which, more importantly, evolves into the perfect, number representative of eternity, i.e., the number **7**—because 4x4= 16= **7**, 13x13= 169= 16= **7**, and 22x22= 484= 16= **7**. And, when we multiply 8x7 we get 56 which equals Annie Pardee, equals **11**. Furthermore, when we examine the numbers <u>**169**</u> and <u>**484**</u> (the products of 13x13, and 22x22) more closely, something miraculous happens—because 16+9= **25** (Annie), and 96+1= **97** (Sarah & Annie Winchester), while 48+4= **52** (Winchester), and 84+4= **88** (the higher dimensional expression of the name Winchester).

Thus, the number **44** not only serves as a higher dimensional expression of Sarah's maiden name, it also emerges as a higher dimensional unification of Sarah, William, and Annie's numerology—and, therefore, functions as a kind of slide rule by which Sarah's numerology can be ciphered. As we have seen, 24 is the foundation of her numerology, but 44 is the *key*. No matter how the numbers are rotated, multiplying them always brings the same result. For example, 20 (Sarah) x 31 (Pardee) = 620= 8= **44**, or, 2x4= 8= **44**, or, 11x4= **44**, or, 2x13= 26= 8= **44**, or, 11x22= 242= 8= **44**, or, 11x13= 143= 8= **44**. Moreover, when we multiply 44x777, we come back, full circle to 34,188= **24**. Again, all things become simplified and more unified from a higher dimensional perspective.

Of course, it doesn't stop there. Because the House is a monument to higher dimensions, Sarah's numerology doesn't just apply to the higher dimensional relationship of names—it is intricately tied into the very nature of existence itself. In Chapters 6 and 7, I discussed the higher dimensional nature of existence through the view given by modern String Theory. Moreover, in Chapter 8, I overviewed the numerology inherent in the mathematics of *quaternions* and *gauge symmetry* as it applies to hyperdimensional dynamics—and that Mrs. Winchester synthesized these dynamics into a more unified view of reality (see page 70).

So the question arises, "was Sarah hip to the meaning of the higher dimensional symmetry implicit in String Theory?" Remarkably, the answer is yes, she had to be. This is where the *Ramanujan Modular function* (the mathematical foundation of String Theory) comes in. The "modular function" has its basis in the "magical number" 24 (see Glossary, page 210). As we have seen, Sarah deliberately SELECTED the number 24 (which becomes expressed, higher dimensionally, as 44) as the foundation of her numerology. Again, this is no accident. The dynamics of higher dimensions (in Superstring Theory) require precisely 24 modes of "conformal symmetry." Moreover, in order to arrive at higher dimensional expressions of the number 24, Sarah, and the String Theorists found it necessary to simplify 24 to the number 8. Thus, the String Theorists add two additional space-time dimensions to arrive at ten dimensions, while Sarah simply multiplies the number 8 by itself, resulting in 64 which then equals ten—or, more importantly, 8 rotates into 44 which, numerologically, is the same difference because 44 multiplied by itself equals 1,936= 19= 10. It is worthy of note that String Theorists do not yet know why the modular function works—they admit "it's as if there is a deep numerology at work in the process."

Although 44 and 51 are different numerological expressions of Sarah's maiden name, the difference between them is always 7. As we shall further see, the difference between 7 and 11 is 13. Moreover, 13 is the higher dimensional, numerological expression of all three Winchesters: Sarah, William, and Annie. 20 (Sarah) multiplied by itself equals 400= 4 which then rotates into **13**. 34 (William) multiplied by itself equals 1,156= **13**. Also note the juxtaposition of the numbers **11** and **56** (11= Sarah, and 56= Annie Pardee). Thus, the numerological expression of William (34), multiplied by itself results in Sarah (11) standing side by side with Annie Pardee (56).

25 (Annie) multiplied by itself equals 625= **13**. Now take a closer look at the number **625**. Notice that 6+25= **31** (Pardee), the mirror image of 13. And 52 (Winchester, also the mirror image of Annie's number 25) multiplied by itself, equals 2,704= **13**—look more closely, **2704** becomes 27+4= **31**. So the name Winchester, multiplied by itself becomes Pardee. Notice the mirror-like shuffling of the numbers. This is a simple but important dynamic of the

rotational symmetry of *quaternions.* Now multiply Pardee (31) by itself—the result is 961. 96+1= **97**= Sarah & Annie Winchester. Is this all mere coincidence? No way. As we shall further see, Sarah used other devices designed to affirm the observer's findings.

It is interesting to note that the standard explanation of the switchback's anomalous characteristics, to this very day, is that "it was built to confuse evil spirits."

The numerological features are present throughout the House. Sarah took great care to display her numerology and the message behind it. The main driveway is lined with 13 palm trees. There are 13 bathrooms, the thirteenth of which has 13 windows. The chandelier in the Ballroom was specially designed to have 13 globes. In the seance room, there are 13 pegs mounted on the wall on which Sarah hung the robes she wore during her seances. Many of the flights of stairs have 13 steps. Sarah's will contained 13 parts, and it was signed by her 13 times. When Sarah died, in 1922, the House had 148 rooms, which, numerologically, equals 13.

In 1906 the great San Francisco earthquake damaged much of the house, the numerological number for that year is 7. Today, the refurbished house has 160 rooms which equals a numerological 7.

In addition to 47 staircases, there are 47 fireplaces throughout the House, 13 of which are wood-burning fireplaces. 47= 11, or, 47 can be viewed separately as the juxtaposition of the numbers 4, 13, and 22 with the number 7. Of course, the 4 (and its rotations) represents Pardee (31) and the 7 represents Winchester (52). 47 multiplied by itself is <u>2,209</u> which equals 13, and, of course, **22+9= 31** (Pardee). 47 minus 13 equals **34** which is the numerological number for the name William. 34 = 7. Also, remember that 47 is equivalent to the name Anne Pardee.

There are 52 skylights in the House. 52 is the numerological number for the name Winchester. 52= 7. 7x7= 49= **13**, while 52x52= 2,704= **13** (and 31). And, of course, 34 (William) x 52 (Winchester) equals 1,768 which equals the master number 22 which then rotates into 4 which rotates back into **13**. Additionally, **1768** (i.e., 17+86) becomes **103**= Sarah Pardee Winchester. Also, note that 52x47 equals 2,444 (the juxtaposition of 24 and 44).

Whenever 7 and 11, or any two combination numbers which rotate into them, are multiplied by themselves, the numerological result is always **13**. Conversely, the result of 13 multiplied by itself, or the combination of any two numbers comprising 13, multiplied by themselves, will always render a numerological **7**.

Needless to say, Sarah's higher dimensional numerology, and all of the ways she displays it, is a never-ending source of revelation.

Prior to the 1906 earthquake, Sarah would occasionally invite some of her neighbors over for ice cream socials. These neighbors were carefully selected by Sarah—the common denominator was that they all had young daughters. From her numerous balconies, Sarah would watch the girls frolicking in the gardens and around the hedges. In essence, she was inviting the girls over to play with Annie.

Mrs. Winchester kept her most prized possessions locked away in a safe. These items included woolen underwear, socks, and fishlines all belonging to William. Other items in the safe included the faded newspaper clipping displaying Annie's obituary, and a small purple, velvet box which contained a lock of her infant hair.

The years following the earthquake marked the final phase of Sarah's life. Having been reduced to only four stories, the House seemed to affirm to Sarah the divine significance of the number 13 (the higher expression of 4) as the supreme number unifying her with William and Annie—existing as a sort of holy trinity.

The elder Mrs. Winchester, of whom it is said, bore a strong physical resemblance to Queen Victoria, became a total recluse, having contact only with her Chinese butler and her niece/secretary, Frances Merriman, upon whom was bestowed the task of conducting business with the outside world. Would-be visitors were turned away with the polite but firm statement, "Mrs. Winchester is not available." Even president Theodore Roosevelt was turned away in such a manner.

It is true that, as a medium, Sarah had an interest in communicating with deceased spirits. That is what her nightly seances were all about. However, contrary to popular belief, she was not conducting the seances to have the spirit world dictate building instructions to her. That's not how the process works—her angel guides would never permit such interference. Her seances had more to do with communicating with William and Annie than anything else. No doubt, Sarah's angel guides inspired her to reach higher insights, just as she inspires us to stretch our intuition beyond all limits. The House is clearly a result of her inspired vision.

As I toured through the Winchester House, I was awestruck by Sarah's remarkable genius. The House is a living work of art. But most importantly, it is an open book beckoning the observer to literally climb the stairs of enlightenment.

I was there for two primary reasons. First, I wanted to unlock the mystery of this monument to higher dimensional consciousness. And, second, I wanted to see if I could gain any further understanding of the mystery by communicating with Sarah's spirit. I hadn't yet reached the third insight which involves understanding the *ultimate* message implicit in the number 13.

So, after completing the tour, I decided to come back the next day. I didn't sleep much that night. My mind was bulging with the intricacies of the mystery. Not only was Sarah ahead of her time, she was ahead of our time.

The following day found me back in the House. As I passed by the stairs leading to the ceiling and the doors which open into solid walls, I envisioned Sarah peering into hyperdimension through these portals. Likewise, I could see her higher dimensional architecture, conspicuously displayed throughout the House, in the form of her "upside-down" columns—the theme was remarkably consistent with M.C. Escher's *Doric Columns* (Figure 1.)—here, the distinction between up and down planes simply dissolve when viewed from a higher dimensional perspective.

Sarah also saw a special purpose in the physical act of ascending and descending every step and stair in the house, even though such activity was not conducive to her severe arthritic condition. As I walked up and down the staircases, I couldn't help but compare the exercise to the process of

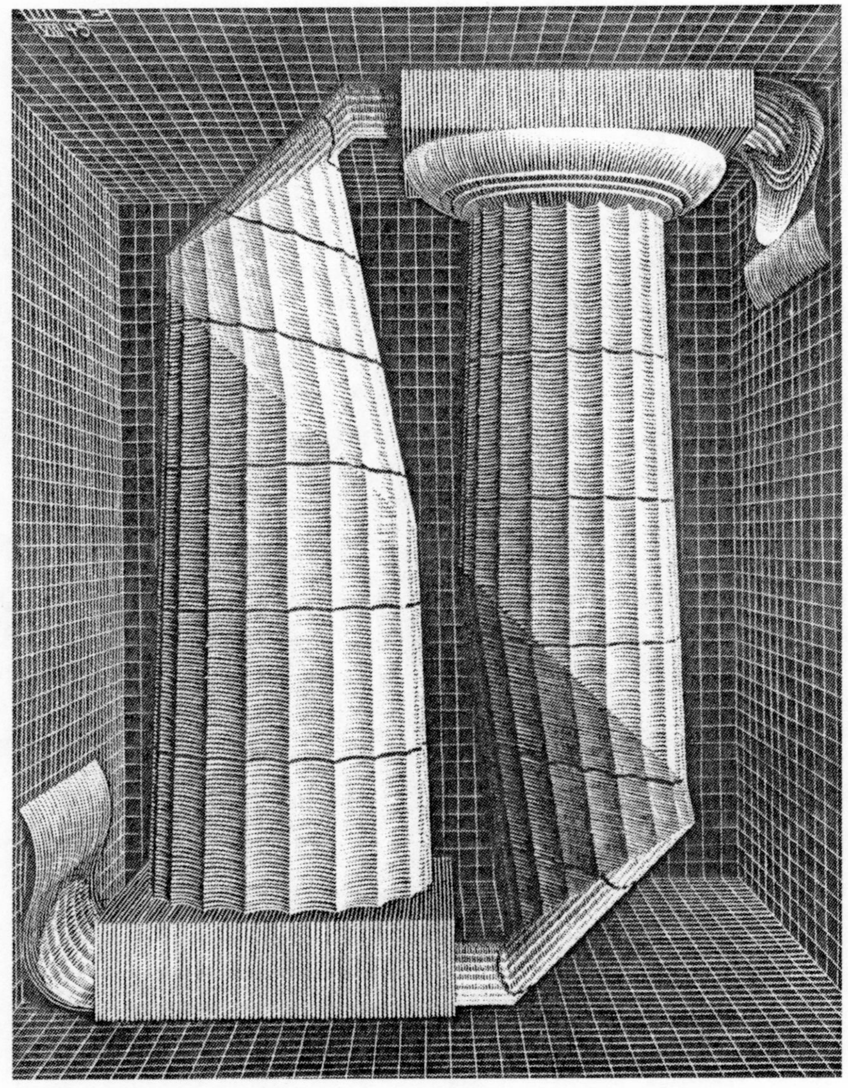

Figure 1

**Doric Columns**
By M.C. Escher

living and learning. We all have to personally walk the stairs of our life's pathways. Some will be easy, some will be hard, some will take us up, some will take us down. If we don't *do* the walking, we won't learn. This is especially true of the intuitive stair-climbing discussed earlier.

Just like life, traversing the labyrinthine passageways of the House sometimes requires walking down a flight of stairs and then walking up another flight of stairs in order to get from one room to another. In one such place, two separate rooms are joined by walking down seven steps and then walking up another eleven steps. Not only are the number of steps designed to capture our attention, but Sarah threw in another tantalizing feature for good measure: the stairs are ingeniously constructed so as to join together in the configuration of the letter Y, which, numerologically, corresponds to the number 7.

I walked down the seven steps and then back up the other eleven steps, gaining only four steps in the process ... or did I? This, in fact, is another revelatory clue to unlocking the mystery.

When Sarah walked down 7 steps and then walked up another 11 steps, she didn't gain four steps—she gained 13 ... in a higher dimension. Here lies one of Sarah's most important signposts leading to a heightened understanding that 13 is the higher synthesis of 7 and 11. This is where the third insight struck me like a bolt of lightning. It took the actual walking of the stairs to affirm the essential relationship of the numbers, and, what that relationship represented. Now I understood the synthesis to a much higher degree—but there was still another step to go. My third insight needed additional validation, and, like an irresistible force, I found myself summoned back to the Ballroom.

I knew that, somehow, Sarah had to exhibit the number 13 simultaneously, between the numbers 7 and 11, in a higher dimensional way that would transcend the wildest expectations of the observer. And, I knew it had to tie in with the two glass window panes displaying the Shakespearean verses.

But how can the two glass windows spontaneously project the numbers 7 and 11 while the number 13 (expressed as 13, instead of 4) is projected between them on a higher dimensional plane? The answer is that all three keys have to fit the lock in unison, rather than one at a time. First, look at the inscriptions. Shakespeare had written eight words into each line. However, Sarah deliberately omitted the first word in each line so that they would both be reduced to 7 words—and, sure enough, that's how both inscriptions appear.

Now observe the position of the two window panes on both sides of the fireplace. Numerologically, the windows can be seen two ways. First, they each appear as the number one. But as we observe them flanking the fireplace in unison, we, in fact, see a widened 11. Second, if we simply add them together, so that 1+1= 2, we still have the numerological 11. Thus, the two windows simultaneously project the numbers 7 and 11.

Additionally, Sarah's two alter egos, Cressida and Richard, who are the respective subjects of each inscription, bear out another numerological attribute which exists as one unified expression between them: Cressida plus Richard equals 13.

But how are we to plainly see the number 13 appear in the middle, between the two glass windows, manifested in such a way that we can actually see it from a higher dimensional perspective? This is exactly what I was thinking as I entered the Ballroom. I also thought about something St. Thomas Aquinas said about attaining knowledge through faith. In essence, what Aquinas meant, is that intuitive knowing and faith rotate into each other—you can't have one without the other. So, I knew that the transcendent expression of the synthesis, embodied in the number 13, was there, hiding in plain sight.

I looked over at the fireplace wall. The two stained-glass windows flanked my periphery, and I looked straight ahead, to the center. And ... there it was, beaming in my face like the Holy Grail. The mirror hanging directly over

**Mirror above mantle in Ballroom reflecting 13-globe chandelier, circa 1928**

Courtesy of The Winchester Mystery House

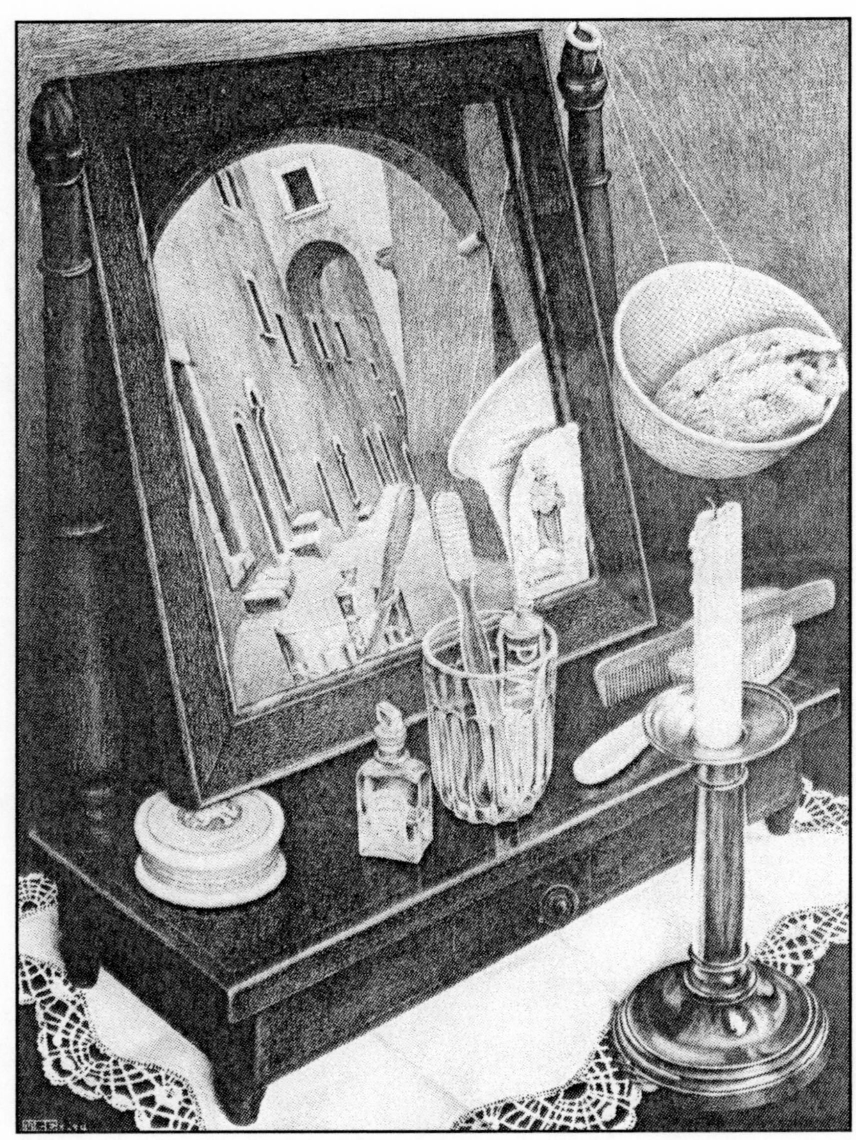

**Still Life with Mirror**

By M.C. Escher

the middle of the mantle, above the fireplace, reflected back a fourth dimensional view of the Ballroom's 13-globe chandelier. M.C. Escher couldn't have drawn it better. It was stunning. It was perfect. It was Sarah's Synthesis exactly the way she wanted us to see it. But it didn't stop there. True to form, Sarah had provided still further affirmations ... just to make sure we had gotten it right.

The image in the mirror brought me back to Sarah's magical number 44. I could now see its greater meaning. The *first 4* in the number represents a fourth higher dimension reflecting back from its source above the mantle. Next, the *second 4*, in its highest expression, appears in the mirrored image of the 13-globe chandelier. Using the numbers exactly as they appear, i.e., 4 and 13, all one has to do is multiply them: 4x13= 52, and 52 equals Winchester. TRULY, THIS IS NO ACCIDENT.

Additionally, the numbers 7, 11, and 13 possess a magical, hyperdimensional quality when they are multiplied, collectively, with any two-digit number. Let's use the number 44 as an example. When 44 is multiplied by the number **7**, we get 539. Now multiply 539 by **11**. The result is 5,929. Now multiply 5,929 by **13**. The number 44 comes back as a higher dimensional, symmetrical expression of itself in the number **44044**.

## Revelations and Affirmations from the "Spiderweb Window"

Revelation and affirmation are the *Yin* and *Yang* of insight—one is not complete without the other. Sarah incorporates this principle in every aspect of her *mystery*—

down to the most intricate detail. For example, the observer will have extreme difficulty comprehending the message implicit in the "switchback staircase" without, first, achieving the fundamental insight to be derived from perusing the Ballroom ceiling.

Sarah designed her mystery in such a way as to lead the enlightened observer from one level of insight up to another, and another, etc. It's truly a matter of peeling back layer upon layer—probing deeper and deeper. And, just when you think you have it all figured out, you find there are still more layers to fathom. But that's the nature of insight and revelation—in its most pristine form, it is *never ending*. Sarah knew that! She also knew that once we made our way through "all" of the layers (or, at least what appears to be all of the layers), we would eventually wind up in the thirteenth bathroom. Not to be facetious, let's call it the "bathroom of understanding."

The thirteenth bathroom has thirteen windows. The *spiderweb windows* were specially designed by Sarah (see Figure 2).

To the casual observer, the spiderweb window is a strange, yet beautiful construction of glass and metal. However, unlike most of the insight provoking features throughout the House, the meaning of the spiderweb window will not be revealed unless the observer understands the message intrinsic in all of the other "revelatory signposts."

The "switchback staircase" may serve as the *primer*, but the spiderweb window, thus named because of its peculiar spiderweb design, *is* Sarah's numerological "Rosetta Stone." It also functions as *the affirmation* of affirmations.

Figure 2

**Spiderweb Window**

Courtesy of The Winchester Mystery House

Although it is beautiful and intriguing, the spiderweb window is not nearly as obvious as all of the other anomalous features throughout the House. Sarah wanted us to recognize exactly what we were looking at, with just a cursory glance.

The spiderweb design is significant for several reasons. For one thing, it truly possesses the quality of captivating those who venture in. But more importantly, it represents the tangled, interconnectedness of all things—these are not just geometric lines intersecting a plane of glass, rather these are living strands of fibrous string which not only connect the individual pieces of glass, but also, through the dynamics of *gauge symmetry,* they unify *all things* into a complete whole. That concept, in itself, is revealing.

But what else are we to see in this window? Sarah knew we would immediately notice that the outside perimeters of this web (unlike the spiderwebs we observe in nature) form a four-sided square. Of course, we are not surprised by that. By now, we expect to see the number four (and its rotations) prominently displayed. In fact, Sarah purposely embedded 4 *(quaternion)* pieces of glass into the outermost edge of each of the four sides just so we wouldn't miss the point. There's no question about it, each of the web's sides has the value of 4, 13, and 22. And, we also know what happens when we add or multiply these numbers. For example, we know that four 4's will give us 16 (or Anne), and four 13's will result in 52 (standard numerology for the name Winchester), and four 22's will render 88 (the higher dimensional expression of Winchester). We recognize and appreciate the important meaning conveyed by those numbers.

However, as we begin to look deeper into the web, we remember that Sarah has a remarkable way of upping the ante. So, with all the anticipation of an Easter egg hunt, we dive in.

The next thing Sarah wants us to notice is that the web contains 49 separate pieces of glass. Since 4+9= 13, we recognize this to be an affirmation of the unifying significance of that number. Also, we recall that 49 is 7 squared.

Of course it doesn't stop there. There has to be more to the number 49 than we know. So we now multiply 4x9, and, sure enough, we get 36 (Anne & Sarah). Next, 49 squared results in <u>2,401</u>. 24 (Sarah Pardee) + 1= 25 (Annie). Moreover, by reversing the numbers in 2,401, we get 10+24= 34 (William), or, 10+42= 52 (Winchester). Thus, Sarah has already succeeded in showing us that 49 is another number that unifies her with Annie and William. But let's take it a step further by multiplying 49x11. The result is 539. 5+39= 44 (the highest expression of Sarah Pardee). Now multiply 49x44, the product is 2,156.

21+56= 77 (Annie Winchester). And, 49x22= 1,078. 10+78= 88 (the highest expression of Winchester). Sarah had good reason to emphasize the unifying power of 49.

Next, Sarah wants to direct our attention to the number 52 (Winchester). But where is it? No matter how we count the pieces of glass, we cannot find 52. Ahh yes… we have to look in-between the pieces of glass. Sure enough, there it is. The glass pieces are all joined together at 52 different points. As we have seen, 52 multiplied by itself results in 2,704. When these numbers are added together, the sum is **13**. And when we add 27+4, the result is **31** (Pardee) which is the mirror image of 13. Moreover, 13+31= 44 (the highest expression of Sarah Pardee).

We also remember that the mirror image of 52 (Winchester) is 25 (Annie), and when we multiply 52x25, we get 1,300, or 13. And when 52 is multiplied by 11 (Sarah), the result is 572, which becomes 5+72= 77 (Annie Winchester). Furthermore, 52x22= 1,144 which is the juxtaposition of 11 (Sarah) and 44 (Sarah Pardee), and when we multiply 11x44, the result is 484, which then becomes 48+4= 52, or 84=4= 88.

At the core of the web, we see a small circle. It is the only circle within the square. The circle is not intersected or divided in any way, nor does it have any of the weblike characteristics we see distributed over the rest of the window's surface. Yet, everything seems to lead to the circle, and everything emanates from it. There appear to be two, distinct, spiderweb rings flowing outward from the circle like concentric waves in a pond. Their spiderweb quality is the result of inverting all of the arcs which connect the sixteen circular points of each ring. Moreover, each of the rings appear to have been assigned the numeric value of 16—a property shared by a third, squared-off ring which forms the outer boundaries of the web.

Of course, we are aware that 16 is the numerological number for Anne. We also know that 16 simplifies to 7. So, how shall we make sense of this obvious display of numbers? Since we have already counted the pieces of glass, we know that 16x3= 48, plus 1 (the circular, middle piece) equals 49, which simplifies to 13. And, 4x9= 36 (Anne & Sarah). Moreover, 16 multiplied by itself results in 256, which is the juxtaposition 2 (Sarah) and 56 (Annie Pardee), and, when we add 25+6, we get 31 (Pardee).

With all that said, we focus on the number 7 (16 simplified). Here (in the 3 outer concentric rings), we see 777 (William Wirt Winchester). Sarah provided the number 49 so that we could affirm our observations. She knew that we would multiply 777x49, which then equals 38,073. Now we simply add 38+73, and we get 111, which is the conventional numerology for William (34), Wirt (25), Winchester (52). Naturally, Sarah doesn't stop there. We are lavished, still, with more affirmations. Knowing that 49 simplifies to 13, we now multiply 13x777. The result is 10,101, or, 111. And, of course, when we multiply the mirror image of 13, i.e., 31 (Pardee) x 777, we get the identical effect in 24,087. 24+87= 111. It is also worthy of note that 11x1= 11 (Sarah). Thus, 4, or any number which rotates into 4 (or, more precisely, any rotation of the name Pardee), multiplied by 777 will always render 111.

Sarah further knew we would then apply the tables of our thoughts to the number 52. So, we now multiply 52x777, resulting in 4,0404 (444), the juxtaposition of 44 and 4. Now we simply multiply 44x4, which gives us 176, which becomes 76+1= 77 (Annie Winchester). Also, notice that when we multiply the mirror image of 52, i.e., 25 (Annie) x 777, we get the same result: 19,425, 19+ 425= 444. Furthermore, when we multiply 34 (William) x 777, the outcome is 26,418, which becomes 26+418= 444. Thus, any rotation of the number 7, multiplied by 777, will result in 444. However, 7 (expressed as 7) multiplied by 777 will not conform to the same symmetry.

Here is where the spiderweb's deeper meaning becomes more evident. When we view the circle in the middle of the web as a fourth, integrating principle, which has the power, in essence, to manifest whatever numerical value is needed to fulfill or complete a given symmetry, we are gaining a glimpse of its higher meaning. This is where gauge symmetry appears to emerge—transcending the realm of quaternions.

Within the web's structure, different, yet intricately related four-dimensional symmetries are at work. However, none of the symmetries can exist without the unifying power of the circle. Moreover, because of the circle's monistic nature, any numerical value derived from it, in order to integrate a given symmetry, will not be duplicated. That is why the symmetry of the 777 group is broken when we try to multiply it by 7. The value derived from the circle must be variant from the numbers in the symmetrical group. Thus, when we multiply 777 by any rotation of 7 (*instead of 7*), we will then get the desired 444 symmetry—for example, if we treat the value of the circle as 52 (a variant of 7), and multiply it by 777, we get 4,0404= 444, or, 34x777=26,418 which becomes 26+418= 444. Conversely, when we treat the value of the circle as 13 (which is not equivalent with 7), and multiply it by 777, we get 10101, or, the 111 *symmetry*. Likewise, any rotation of 13 will achieve the same result, e.g., 49x777= 38,073, which becomes 38+73= 111, etc.

Another important feature of the spiderweb window Sarah wants the observer to notice is that each of its four sides forms a triangular shape, pointing to the circular center (see Figure 3). We count out 12 glass pieces in each triangle. However, the four triangles are not complete unless their points merge, invisibly, into the circle. Then, we see the triangles all sharing the 13th circular piece. We also remember that 13x4= 52 (Winchester).

Ultimately, the meaning of spiderweb window transcends the monistic, spiritual unity of the Winchester trinity—Sarah knew that. Her metaphor of the web, with its concentric wavelike rings of intricately connected strings, conforming to the remarkable, interchanging symmetries of a higher dimensional design, bear an amazing resemblance to the dynamics of String Theory. Was Sarah cognizant of a ten-dimensional existence? Of course she was.

Modern String Theorists, for some inexplicable reason, tend to forget that Pythagoras was the first String Theorist. The concept of existence, derived from the vibrations of a string, structured from a symmetry arising from the number 10, originated with him.

It is clear that Sarah's architecture, numerology, and spirituality are greatly touched by the Pythagorean influence—the spiderweb window is manifest testament to that. The overwhelming application of the number 4 (in all of its forms) is the most salient clue. The outer edges of the spiderweb window display 44 and 44. Added together, we have 88. There is a strong resemblance between the under-

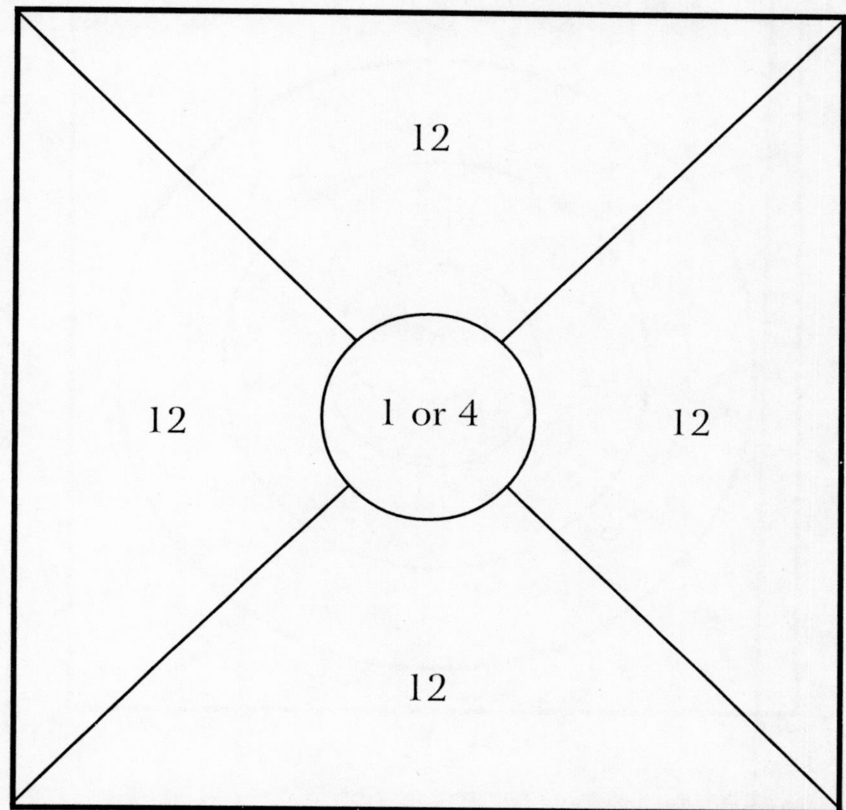


**Figure 3**

## Spiderweb Window

*Four triangles (from each side) converge on the center of the Spiderweb Window. Each triangle has 12 glass pieces, yet the triangles are not complete without the center piece. In order for the triangles to be complete, the circle in the center must provide the value of one or four, whereby, each of the four triangles achieves the value of 13. 4 x 13 = 52 = Winchester.*

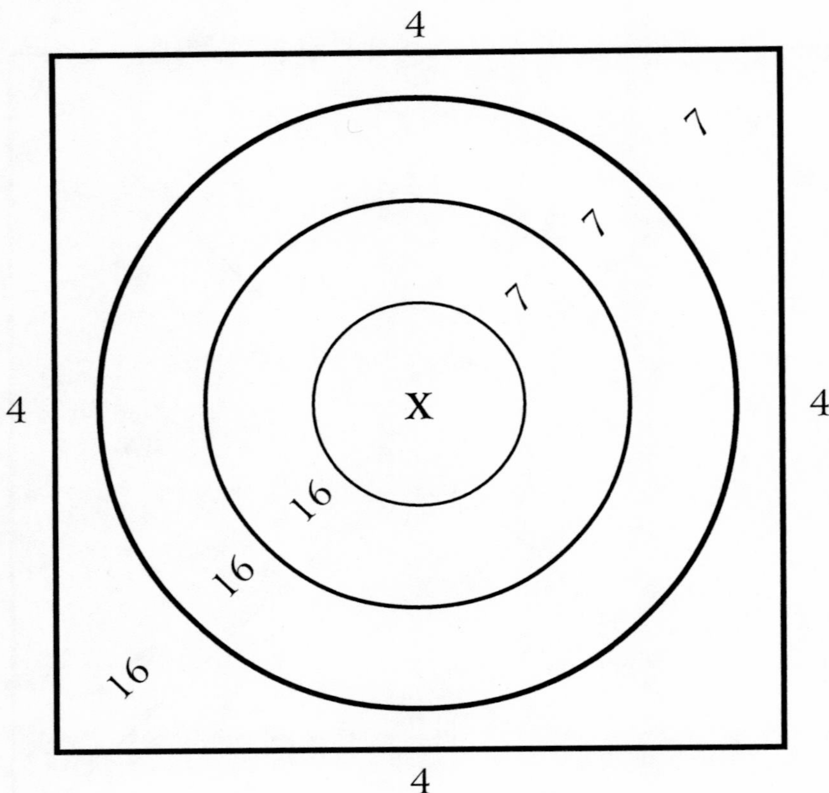


**Figure 4**

## Spiderweb Window

*The concentric outer rings emanating from the center, each have a value of 16 or 7. The four sides of the window have a value of 4, which becomes 44 and 44. The center circle has the power to manifest whatever numeric value is required to complete a given symmetry. For example: if the circle assumes the value of 52, and is multiplied by 777, the result is 40,404, or 444. If the circle assumes the value of 13, and is multiplied by 777, the result is 10,101, or 111.*

lying symmetry of Sarah's 88 and the E(8) x E(8) symmetry inherent in String Theory.

And what of the number 10? This is, perhaps Sarah's best kept secret. For Pythagoras, 4 rotates into 10 by the simple addition of 1+ 2+ 3+ 4 (equals 10). Sarah's higher dimensional numerology had little choice but to lead her to the same place. However, the number 10 was something Sarah chose not to openly display. Like four, 8 was an important number to her. Numerologically, she was compelled to multiply 8x8, thus arriving at 64, which then becomes 10. Moreover, the number 52 had to have been expressed more highly as 5x2= 10, while 44x44 results in 1,936= 19= 10. Furthermore, 52x13= 676= 19= 10, or 52x4= 208= 10. And, finally, when we simply add 49+52 we get 101, which is 11 (Sarah) with a circle in its middle. It also forms the juxtaposition of 10 and 1. 10x1 equals 10. Yes, Sarah was well familiar with the ramifications of Pythagoras' "sacred number" 10.

In the final analysis, 10 numerologically simplifies to *one*. In its purest form, the power of ONE is the true essence of the circle in the middle of Sarah's spiderweb. The truth is always simple. And the simple truth is that all things are unified when they are *one*. Such is the nature of divinity. Whether we call it The Holy Spirit, the Divine Mind, or God, it is all *one*.

Two years after Sarah's death, the renowned magician Harry Houdini came to the Winchester House for a specially arranged midnight seance. He sought to instantly invoke the presence of Sarah's spirit as if he could conjure her up like one of his tricks—with the expectation that she would freely pour out her secrets to him—without his having to earn it. However, as she had been in life, so she was in death—Mrs. Winchester was not available.

Disappointed, Houdini exited the House failing in his attempt to receive a message from Sarah's departed soul. But his real failure was in not recognizing that the message he was seeking had been there all along, staring him in the eye. Sarah had masterfully done her part. Through her mystery—her art—she had created a microcosmic model for confronting the Divine Mystery.

Houdini, like most people, expected revelation to come to him passively, on a silver platter, as though he were a spectator waiting for revelation to magically appear all by itself—simply because he had snapped his fingers in summons. Somehow, he failed to realize that revelation requires active participation—it doesn't just come to *us*, we have to seek *it* out and discover it. It's ironic that as the world's greatest magician, he neglected to see that real "magic" (self-discovery) comes from within.

We must all climb the stairs of our intuition to gain insight—only then will we come face to face with revelation.

As I exited the House, I knew there was no need to seek further contact with Sarah's spirit. Communication with the deceased is born out of the spirit's need to impart to us important information, rather than engage in idle chit chat.

Sarah had already succeeded in telling me all I needed to know. Besides, she was, and still is there, in the most profound way ... amongst the angels hidden in the architecture.

Overview of The Winchester House

Courtesy of The Winchester Mystery House

**Sarah Pardee Winchester**

Courtesy of The History Museums of San Jose

**William Wirt Winchester**

Courtesy of The History Museums of San Jose

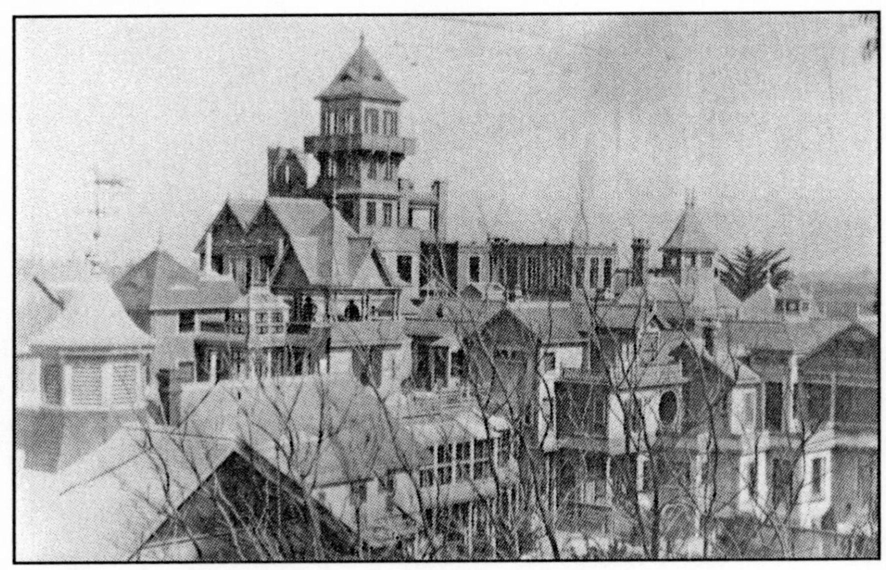

**Original Seven-Story Wincester House**

Courtesy of The Winchester Mystery House

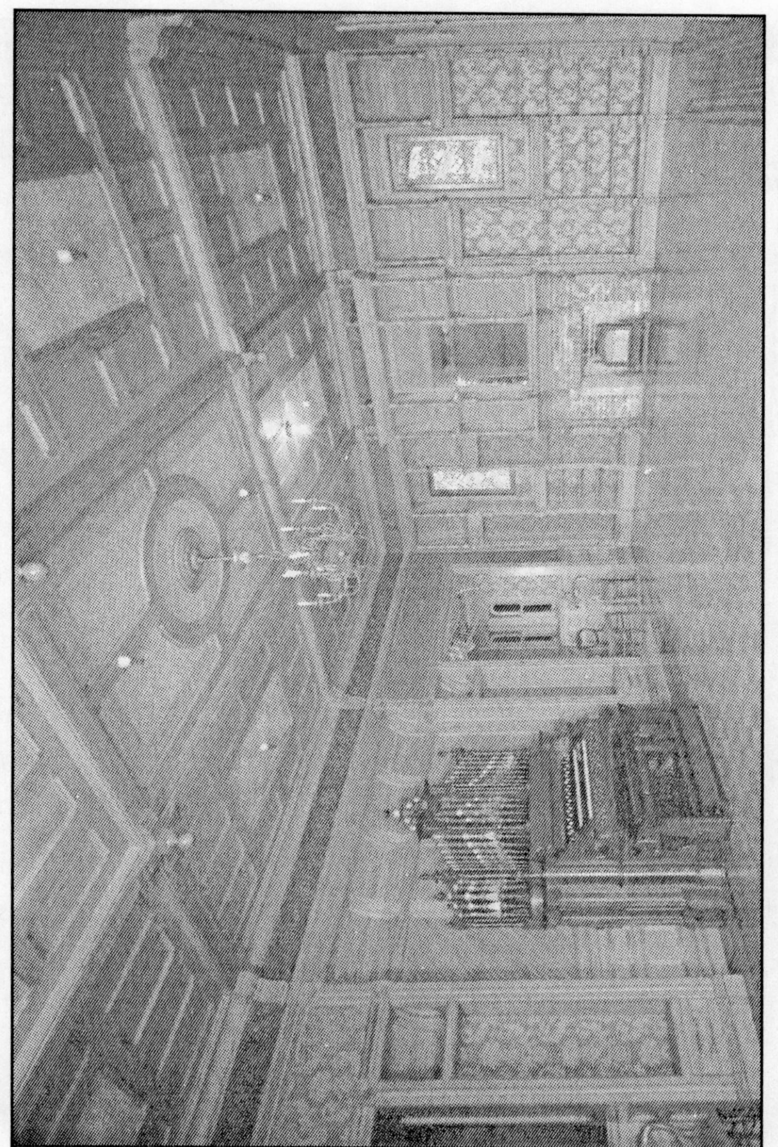

**Grand Ballroom**

Courtesy of The Winchester Mystery House

**Switch-back Staircase**

Courtesy of The Winchester Mystery House

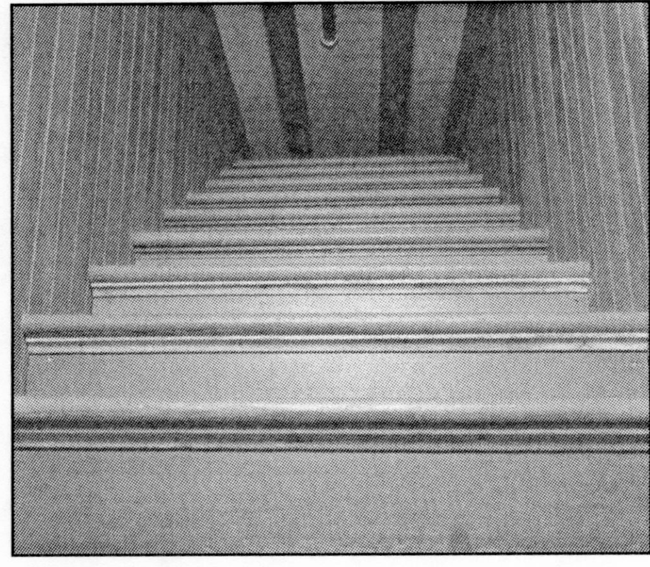

**Stairs Leading to the Ceiling**

Courtesy of The Winchester Mystery House

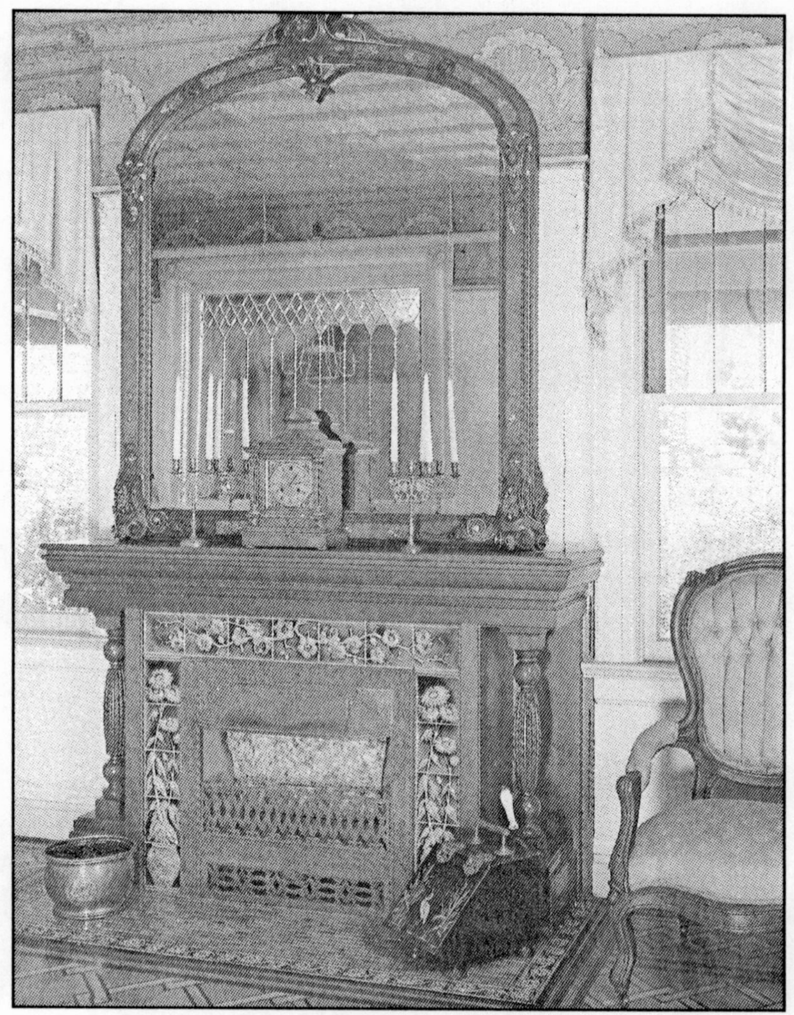

**Mirror above mantle in the Parlor**

Courtesy of The Winchester Mystery House

Notice the two candelabrums reflecting in the mirror above the mantle. Each candelabrum is designed to hold three candles, but there are only two candles mounted in each. When we observe the candles and their reflections in the mirror, we, in fact, see Sarah's magical number 44.

# 21

# THE BIGGER PICTURE

***Why does this magnificent applied science which saves work and makes life easier bring us so little happiness? The answer runs: Because we have not yet learned to make sensible use of it.***

Albert Einstein

ONE HOT AFTERNOON, while writing this book, a scientist friend, Carl, from Cal Tech, joined me for lunch. As we sat in the shade, drinking iced tea, Carl's usual staid expression metamorphosed into droll animation.

"You know," he said, "back at the lab, we're making some major breakthroughs in A I [artificial intelligence]. The day is coming, in the not too distant future, when we will all be obsolete. We're going to be replaced by machines that will be able to out-think us."

I was amazed that he misunderstood the nature of media, and that he had such low regard for human beings as to think of them as being inferior to machines.

I responded, "If I didn't know you better, I would say you are describing the ludicrous, infantile, vision of 'The Matrix' [the motion picture]. How will these super machines achieve consciousness? After all, consciousness is what makes us human; it is the prime ingredient of the life force that is at the core of the soul."

Carl pondered my remarks for a moment. "Damn it," he snorted, "you're introducing variables that can't be quantified or tested [in a laboratory]."

It wasn't my intention to prick such a sensitive chord with my friend. The vulnerability of his scientific precepts had suddenly become exposed like an unsightly wart. It wasn't my fault that consciousness and the life force aren't quantifiable or testable through empirical observation. No, this is a fault of science.

Not to be outdone, my scientist friend tried a different approach. "Well," he said, "I guess it all depends on how we define consciousness."

Carl's somewhat, cocky comment reminded me of something I had just read from Dean Radin (Director of the Consciousness Research Laboratory at the University of Nevada, Las Vegas). Coincidentally, I had Dr. Radin's book, *The Conscious Universe,* in my briefcase. I extracted the book and quoted some of Radin's words:

> **We will see that because scientists are also human, the process of evaluating scientific claims is not as pristinely rational or logical as the general public believes... The tendency to adopt a fixed set of beliefs and defend them to the death is incompatible with science, which is a loose confederation of evolving theories in many domains. Unfortunately,**

> **this tendency has driven some scientists to continue to defend outmoded, inaccurate worldviews ... but history amply demonstrates that science progresses mainly by funerals, not by reason and logic alone** (Radin, 1997).

Carl's demeanor grew defensive. His upper lip began to twitch. "I know when I'm right and when I'm wrong," he retorted. "I'm not one of those dinosaur, hardliners with tunnel vision. So, go ahead, answer me. What's your idea of consciousness?"

I responded, "Do you honestly believe there is a gene for the soul, or for life, or for consciousness?"

"No," he conceded, "but we're not talking genetics; we're talking artificial intelligence, and, so far, you're not answering my question."

"Well then," I replied, "just substitute the word gene for the word microchip—there can never be a microchip for the soul, or the life force, and, as for consciousness, there is an important aspect which is the most essential element of consciousness, and that is *intuition*. Intuition is a function of the soul, not machines. And, as we both know, *artificial intelligence* is a slick term for an advanced computer system which, at best, will only *simulate* the ability to create its own thoughts. The creative process belongs to the domain of intuition, not logic. Logic, by its nature, is subject to conversion into digitalized technology. But there is no way that intuition can be digitalized, neither can it be programmed. All computer technology, including artificial intelligence, is, and always will be, the product of *programmed, digitalized, logical systems*. Such systems may, ultimately, become capable of simulating emotion in that they will be able to *think out* an emotional response or outcome, but they will never *feel* the emotion. It's like playing a CD of Richard Pryor telling a joke—the system's simulation of the process will be rendered perfectly, it may even comprehend the linguistic meaning of the words, but it still will not comprehend the intuitive insights behind the words that, spontaneously, make them funny. Because A I systems will be incapable of *feeling,* they will never know or comprehend the most important thing of all—they will never know *love*. Thus, artificial intelligence will never know God. There can never be a *program* for intuition; therefore, there can never be a microchip for intuition or insight. Artificial intelligence may mechanically simulate the process of living, but it will never be *alive*."

Needless to say, the argument abruptly ended on that note, and our conversation shifted to other topics.

Later, that day, back home, I reflected on my conversation with Carl. I remembered how the late Marshall McLuhan (professor of education at the University of Toronto) warned that misunderstanding media would lead to its misuse. All media, according to McLuhan, is an extension of ourselves. For example, all forms of transportation are media because they are extensions of the function of our feet. Clothing and housing are media because they are extensions of our skin. And all of the technologies that provide us with information are media because they are an extension of our central nervous systems. Thus, the media of computers, and, eventually, artificial intelligence, no matter how remarkable and powerful they become, will still only be extensions of our own brains—ultimately, that's all that such media can ever be. But can humanity be content with that?... Probably not! Not until the human race can spiritually mature to a point where it no longer feels the need to compete with God.

As we humans push bravely into the twenty-first century, we are like the child who rebels against its parent, trying to act out the parental role. Through our media and technology we seek to create a surrogate parent, more to our childish understanding and liking—in the image of our materialistic toys. This reminds me of something another friend once told me: "When God created the universe, he at least knew what he was doing. We [humans], on the other hand, haven't the slightest idea what the hell we're doing. We hardly understand what space, time, and matter are—and everything beyond that is a complete mystery. What the hell makes us think we can play God?"

The great minds of Plato, Einstein, Jung, et al., knew well the restrictions that space-time places on the physical properties of the human brain (not the soul). They knew that perceptions of the brain are always in a state of flux—a process of becoming or unbecoming. Because of its attachment to space-time, the human brain can never have awareness of a *present tense*. Therefore, it can never give us a true perception of *reality*. The best our limited, space-time, brains (organic or mechanized) can ever render is what Plato called "the shadows on the wall." A shadow is only a flat, darkened, two-dimensional, *vacant* image of an object which is illuminated, and three-dimensional—this is analogous to how our brains vacantly try to perceive the reality of higher dimensions. What is vacant or missing is the reality of the present. Thus, the brain sees only illusion.

Einstein said, "People like us, who believe in physics, know the distinction between past, present, and future is only a stubbornly persistent illusion."

Jung proclaimed:

> **The psyche's attachment to the brain, i.e., its space-time limitation, is no longer as self-evident and incontrovertible as we have hitherto been led to believe... so we are not entitled to conclude from the apparent space-time quality of our perception that there is no form of existence *without* space and time. It is not only permissible to doubt the absolute validity of space-time perception; it is, in view of the available facts, even imperative to do so** (Jung, 1960).

Consciousness emanating from the context of space-time presents a paradox. Within the limitations of space-time, the brain is incapable of knowing the reality of *the present*; if that were not so, Heisenberg's uncertainty principle wouldn't be so certain. Only "discontinuous time" is immune to time paradoxes.

Plato told us that the soul (not the brain) lives in the eternal present (or discontinuous time), and therefore, it is only through the process of the soul (or psychic process) that we can know the true nature of reality. Discontinuous time exists outside of space-time in the hyperdimension.

Our illusory attachment to space-time wasn't always a fact of life. Through his visions, Edgar Cayce revealed that, long ago, the human spirit had no attachment to the physical realm of space-time. The implements of our higher faculties, i.e., telepathy, psychokinesis, precognition, clairvoyance, clairsentience, clairaudience, etc., were well intact—we were spiritually mature.

But gradually, as we experimented with the seductive sensuality inherent in the material world, we became insidiously *attached* to its limited structure. We became "encased" in the corporeal shells we now call bodies. Thus, over time, we devolved into spiritual adolescence, losing most of our psychic attributes and spiritual mastery. We were no longer oriented toward spiritual consciousness, instead, we had become prisoners of a self-imposed exile, subjugated by ego consciousness. Hence, life transformed into a struggle for *liberation* which could only be attained through the creative process we now refer to as death.

It is no wonder that Hildegard says (to put it mildly), "The angels are amazed by us." Angels don't possess the ability to choose their destinies (for better or worse) the way that humans do.

William Jennings Bryan (1896) stated the matter eloquently:

> **Destiny is not a matter of chance—it is a matter of choice.**

We humans chose to digress into a destiny attached to space-time. And we continue to reinforce that choice as we sacrifice our true spiritual nature on the altar of a mechanized god, fashioned by our own hands, in the image of our materially obsessed science and technology. That is not to say that technology and science are bad. They are wonderful extensions of ourselves. The problem is that through our misuse of them, they have become the shadows on the walls of our understanding—such shadows reflect back a dark, vacant image of ourselves—they show us how much we have lost.

## Playing God

In the new millennium we look outward towards the starlit heavens. We entertain the notion that, one day, we will become the masters of all that we see. Yet, we don't even see ourselves; we see only our shadows. How are we to master anything if we don't first achieve self-mastery?

Like stubborn children, we hold tightly to the naive belief that through bigger science, bigger technology (i.e., bigger space-time extensions of ourselves), and, bigger power, the power of the *Planck energy* to be precise (10 to the 19th power, billion electron volts), we can triumph over space-time. We already have our sights set on such a venture. However, it will never be the way we envision it.

To start, we would have to develop technology that would enable space travel at extremely high velocities. But as we have already seen, approaching the velocity of light is infinitely impractical, if not impossible. Even if the impossibility of traveling at the speed of light were possible, in human terms, it would still take an eternity to reach most of the star systems and galaxies in our universe. Ahh, but what about inter-dimensional travel via some kind of warp drive as depicted in *Star Trek.* There are two fundamental problems with this approach. First, warping or folding space would require the use of unimaginable energy such as the *Planck energy*. This would be roughly equivalent to the energy of The Big Bang. So, good luck with that! Second, even if we could miraculously produce such energy, and thereby succeed in folding space, we would then be faced with another problem that the writers of science fiction are either unaware of or are conveniently ignoring—folding space would result in obliterating the very stars, galaxies, and solar systems we would be trying to reach. Just imagine the space of our solar system being folded up, flat as a pancake. We would be annihilated. Third, cosmologists, such as Stephen Hawking, see inter-dimensional travel as something which might be attainable by journeying through tunnels in the fabric of space, created by *black holes* called *wormholes* or *Einstein-Rosen bridges*. Such tunnels in space would lead us into other kinds of space in … other *parallel universes*. In fact, Hawking believes there could be an infinite number of parallel universes. As interesting and imaginative as the idea of parallel universes may be, it is not likely that we, or any of our descendants, will ever experience such theoretical phenomena, or know whether or not they even exist; hence, I fail to see any relevance in the idea. The universe we know and live in is more than enough to contend with.

Considering the limitations intrinsic in both humans and space-time, playing God will ultimately prove to be futile. We are certainly justified to wonder how other (alien) beings in the universe might have dealt with the matter.

Carl Sagan's *Contact* offers a sophisticated, sci-fi rendition of what it would be like for the human race to receive a cosmic message from highly evolved beings from another part of the universe. With the use of a mathematical language, Sagan's advanced beings, called "Vegans," send us a schematic diagram showing how to build a gigantic, mechanical contraption which would allow us to transport back to them an individual ambassador representing our primitive, human culture.

Upon construction, the mechanical device, resembling an enormous gyroscope with a gantry suspended overhead, stands poised to drop a pod, containing our ambassador, down through a network of counter-revolving (apparently electromagnetic) rings. The countdown commences, five, four, three, two, one, and ... "drop." Our ambassador, "Dr. Eleanor Arroway," who is hooked up with a mini video-cam, relays back the blow-by-blow details of the mission. However, the control center receives only a broken, garbled picture which quickly degrades into pure static.

Dr. Arroway appears to accelerate through a kind of wormhole which emerges into the "Vegan" star system. Somehow, she finds herself gently touching down on a beautiful beach, or, so it seems. It becomes clear that the images she sees around her are really mental projections. She is in another dimension. But it isn't a dimension of space or time—it is a dimension of Mind. From the opposite side of the "mind beach" a "Vegan" ambassador emerges, appearing, at first, as a sort of fuzzy, being of light. But as he draws nearer, he assumes the image and persona of Dr. Arroway's deceased father. He explains that the images she is perceiving are meant to help her feel more at ease as she tries to comprehend her experience. He gently infers that the human race isn't ready to deal with the transcendent revelation of existence. Such revelation will gradually come to us in "small moves." With that, Dr. Arroway instantly finds herself thrust back to the earthly realm, in the pod, at the bottom of the transport device.

Throughout her debriefing, Dr. Arroway has difficulty describing her *experience*. In fact, her inquisitors refuse to believe her. They flagrantly point to the "objective" evidence displayed by the multifaceted, video record of "the drop," which simply shows the pod descending to the ground, in a fraction of a second. Her account of what took place during the drop doesn't jive with the empirical data, and her insistence that what she experienced was *real* falls on deaf ears. However, there is an anomalous feature to the record, duly acknowledged by one government official. The recording from Dr. Arroway's videocam shows nothing but static—but that's not what's interesting—"what's interesting," is that her videotape shows nearly eighteen hours of static.

What I find interesting is that throughout Carl Sagan's scientific career, he remained a steadfast empiricist. But his final legacy to us, in *Contact* (prior to his death), reveals an uncanny insight into the ultimate conflict between true reality, reflected through the unfettered, human spirit, and the empirical dogma reflected by our attachment to space-time.

Dr. Arroway's experience describes the most common elements inherent in *near death experience*. Through artificial means, she has gained access to the hyperdimension. Her eighteen hours of video static, translated into a split second, reflect an unwitting, space-time affirmation of the *eternal present*, i.e., *discontinuous time*. In that fraction of a second, she has, inadvertently, experienced contact with the Divine Mind through her angel guide (in the guise of a Vegan). Basically, what the being of light is saying when he tells Dr. Arroway that humans must make "small moves" is that we haven't yet reached spiritual maturity.

The Vegans or, for that matter, any highly evolved beings would, at some point in their development, come to realize the greater reality that transcends the material realm of space-time. Therefore, they would have evolved beyond the need for physical bodies, ego consciousness, and death. If we seek to find such highly evolved beings in space-time, we're looking in the wrong place. Their realm of existence is the synthesis of pure thought—the supreme state of consciousness that merges with the Divine Mind—in some respects, this bears a remarkable resemblance to Pierre Teilhard de Chardin's concept of "The Omega Point."

As for the human race, we collectively chose to attach ourselves to a material existence, and along with it, a materially oriented ego consciousness. Space-time can be a very lonely place; our attachment to it makes us incomplete. It is not surprising, then, that we human beings search for the part of us that is missing. But we are entering a new age of self-discovery. Gradually, through small moves, we are awakening the vacant part of ourselves that has been dormant for so long. We have much to learn, particularly about the unifying power of love.

Fortunately, we are not alone, or cut off from the divine source which gave us life—and also gave us the dreamgate and beings of light to guide us. Moreover, we have the power to choose our own, individual path to enlightenment. We are all powerful, creative beings. The divine river flows through us all. Our true nature, once we reclaim it, knows no limits. We are all part of a much greater whole—a bigger picture through which we are collectively capable of wonders we haven't yet conceived of. And all these things will pass ... through our infinite capacity to love!

# GLOSSARY

**Angels:** Beings of light. The mediums of spiritual existence (page 15).

**Anthropic Principle:** The doctrine which states that the universe is uniquely designed to allow for the existence of living beings—otherwise, we wouldn't be here to observe it. Thus, the physical universe didn't happen by accident or random chance—rather it is the product of deliberate, conscious design (pages 73-76).

**Arrow of Time:** A term first coined by astrophysicist Arthur Eddington to describe the phenomenon of time which has a beginning and moves forward towards an ending (pages 62-64).

**Artificial Intelligence:** Theoretically, any device or means by which the human brain may be artificially extended or replicated (page 194).

**Astral Projection:** The activity through which the soul temporarily leaves the body (See Out of Body Experience).

**Big Bang:** The initial act of creation which marks the beginning of material existence and the development of our universe (page 48).

**Clairaudience:** "Clear hearing." The higher faculty of mediumship through which one hears the telepathic impression of a spirit's temporal voice and speech (page 114).

**Clairsentience:** "Clear feeling." The higher faculty of mediumship through which one feels the telepathic impression of a spirit's emotions and tactile memories (page 114).

**Clairvoyance:** "Clear seeing." The higher faculty of mediumship through which one sees the telepathic impression of a spirit's temporal body and visual memories (page 114).

**Conservation of Energy and Mass:** The law of science that states that physical energy (or its equivalent in mass) can neither be created nor destroyed (page 61).

**c velocity:** The velocity of light. The supreme speed limit of the material universe (page 41).

**Death:** The transition of the soul from material, space-time existence to spiritual existence in the hyperdimension (pages 53-54).

**Discontinuous Movement:** An instantaneous action in which no movement occurs. The speed of thought (page 28).

**Discontinuous Time:** An interval having no beginning or ending. The *eternal now* (page 28).

**Divine Mind:** The dynamic essence of the God process. The source of all existence (page 54).

**Doppler Effect:** The relationship between frequency and speed, particularly as it relates to the movement of stars and galaxies seen through their blue-shifted or red-shifted spectra. Blue shift equals higher frequencies which are moving closer, while red shift equals lower frequencies which are moving farther away. With the Doppler effect, Edwin Hubble showed that the predominant red shift observable in all parts of the universe proved that it is expanding outward away from its original point of inception (page 62).

**Dreamgate:** The process by which the soul (during the dream state) temporarily takes leave of the dimensions of space-time to access the hyperdimension (pages 77-82).

**Ego Consciousness:** The illusion of "self" created by attachment to material, space-time existence (page 132).

**Electromagnetic Force:** The force that arises between particles having electric charge. The second strongest of the four fundamental forces.

**$E=mc^2$:** Energy is equivalent to mass times the speed of light squared. Einstein's famous equation which serves as the foundation of his Special Theory of Relativity (page 42).

**Energy:** The intrinsic force through which all entities, material or spiritual, are dynamic or active.

**Field:** Something that exists throughout space and time, as opposed to a particle that exists at only one point at a time.

**Forgiveness:** The supreme expression of unconditional love—the emancipator of the spirit (pages 125-130).

**Ghosts:** Dispossessed or lost souls who, because of their attachment to material existence and the negative energy of ego consciousness, dwell in a dark, murky kind of limbo which interferes with achieving the enlightened state of consciousness essential to accessing the transcendent, spiritual existence of the hyperdimension (page 132).

**God:** The Divine Mind. The source and cause of all existence.

**God Process:** The supreme unifying principle from which all existence is derived.

**Gravitational Force:** The most universal, long range, yet weakest of the four, fundamental natural forces—having the property of always being attractive, over large distances.

**Heaven:** The supreme state of consciousness—merging with the Divine Mind. Omega consciousness (page 54).

**Heisenberg's Uncertainty Principle:** One can never be certain of both the position and the velocity of a particle; the more accurately one knows the one, the less accurately one can know the other.

**Hell:** The lowest state of consciousness brought about by choosing to be separate and apart from the God process. Alpha worship (page 54).

**Higher Dimensions:** Dimensions of mind and spirit—transcendent of material existence and the confines of four-dimensional space-time.

**Hyperdimension:** The higher dimensions unified as one whole. The transcendent state of spiritual existence (pages 39-55).

**Insight:** Profound revelation induced by the exercise of one's higher intuitive faculties.

**Intuition:** Perfect, spontaneous knowledge which is not invented, and, by its nature, is *a priori* rather than *a posteriori.* The pure basis of all psychic phenomena.

**Imaginary Numbers:** Special numbers which, when calculated (in field equations), make no distinction between space and time (pages 46-47).

**Imaginary Time:** Time (particularly on the quantum level) which has no direction (page 62).

**Kirlian Effect:** A scientific technique in which a high frequency, high voltage form of photography captures trace images of the resonant discharge of pure, non-organic, life force energy (pages 86-88).

**Life Force:** Pure spiritual energy. The dynamic, animating essence of the soul.

**Mass:** The quantity of matter in a body; its inertia, or resistance to acceleration. The property of weight (page 41).

**Matter:** Anything which can be influenced or affected by the four natural forces. A construct of energy, derived from the four natural forces, which is bound within a field. The resonant velocity of different kinds of energy within the dimensions of space-time (pages 42-48).

**Media:** Technology which functions as an extension of the human body (page 197).

**Medium:** One whose higher, psychic faculties are sensitive to telepathic communication with spirit beings (page 113).

**NDE (Near-Death Experience):** The experience of surviving clinical death which includes the experience of leaving one's body, and gaining glimpses into the afterlife in the deepest and most profound levels of the hyperdimension (pages 93-104).

**Newtonian Physics:** Concepts about the physical nature of the universe espoused by Isaac Newton—most notably the view that the universe is a static, unchanging machine.

**Numerology:** A system of ciphering the mystical relationship of numbers and letters of the alphabet for the purpose of divining their special or hidden meaning (pages 154-155).

**OBE (Out-of-Body Experience):** The activity through which the soul temporarily leaves the body and accesses the hyperdimension—most commonly through the dreamgate (pages 189-192).

**Ockham's Razor:** The scientific precept which states: all things being equal, the simplest answer to a scientific inquiry is the true one.

**Omega Point:** The doctrine espoused by Pierre Teilhard de Chardin that views all enlightened human souls as one, collective, evolving entity, which, once it achieves the highest point of development, will merge with God (page 205).

**Phantom Leaf Effect:** The phenomenon of Kirlian Photography by which the trace discharge of the soul's non-organic life force can be observed (pages 79-80).

**Planck Energy:** Max Planck's theoretical calculation of a physical energy that was likely to have been present during the Big Bang, i.e., 10 to the $19^{th}$ power GeV (Giga electron volts) (page 201).

**Planck Length:** For practical purposes, the smallest, theoretical measurement of size in the material universe in which the effects of Quantum Field Equations are deemed operable. A size one hundred billion billion times smaller than a proton (page 46).

**Point Particles:** Quantum particles. In Quantum Mechanics, a particle is believed to occupy one point in space at a time (page 59).

**Prime Mover:** The doctrine of St. Thomas Aquinas which is the foundation of his proof of the existence of God (page 57).

**Precognition:** The higher intuitive faculty through which one has present knowledge of space-time events which have not yet occurred in the path of the "arrow of time."

**Prophetic Dreaming:** Precognitive insight acquired while in the dreamgate (pages 83-85).

**Psychic:** Greek word meaning "of the soul." All phenomena pertaining to the higher intuitive faculties.

**Psychometry:** A form of tactile clairvoyance in which the medium or "sensitive" tunes in on a specific resonance by touching an object or person.

**Pure Energy:** Perfect, spiritual (hyperdimensional) energy which cannot be observed or measured because of its immateriality—and, therefore, transcends the energies of the four natural forces bound by four-dimensional space-time (pages xiii, 51-52). See Scott's Pure Energy Hypothesis.

**Pure Thought:** Thought which is perfect and "true," not invented. It is also non-verbal and spontaneous. Pythagoras, Plato, Einstein, Heisenberg, and Jung all recognized that "pure thought" exists as "reality" which transcends the limitations of space-time conceptualization. Pure thought, therefore, resides in the mind of the hyperdimension (page 50).

**Quantum Mechanics:** A theory of microcosmic reductionism which views matter as being made, in essence, of smaller and smaller versions of itself, i.e., particles within particles within particles, etc. The theory, although useful, fails to provide a coherent explanation of what matter is (pages 59-60).

**Ramanujan Modular Function:** The "mystical" mathematics of the East Indian mathematician, Srinivasa Ramanujan, which provides the foundation of modern String Theory. In the modular function, the "magic number" 24 constantly appears in places where it is least expected, miraculously canceling out undesired infinities. For String Theory, this means that each of the 24 modes of the Ramanujan function conforms to a specific vibration generated by the string. The higher dimensional generalization of the number 24 in the modular function simplifies to the number 8. Because physicists include two additional space-time dimensions, the Superstring is expressed as 8+2=10, hence, the origin of the tenth dimension. The string's "self-consistency" requires it to resonate in ten dimensions. String theorists do not yet understand why the modular function works. They admit "it's as if there is some kind of deep numerology at work" in the process.

It is worthy of note that Sarah Winchester also saw a higher dimensional numerology at work in the magic number 24 which she also simplified to varying modes of the number 8 (pages 48, 60, 164) Also see String Theory (page 212 g).

**Remote Viewing:** By accessing the hyperdimension through the dreamgate, one is able to gain a higher dimensional perspective of all things from every vantage point, in the past, present and future tense (page 91).

**Resonance:** The dynamic principle which underlies all energy. Instead of viewing quantum units of energy (particles) as occupying points in space, the essence of matter (through String Theory) can now be seen as varying modes of vibration rather than point particles. Thus, all matter is literally made of a kind of harmonic music.

**Revelation:** Divine insight, usually acquired through the dreamgate, which is intended to serve as an intervening force or influence.

**Second Law of Thermodynamics:** The scientific law which states that in a closed system, order (in the present or past tense) will, over time, turn increasingly into disorder or entropy (in the future tense). The Second Law provides compelling evidence that the material universe (on the macro level) had a beginning, and the fundamental laws governing its nature conform to an "arrow of time" (page 62).

**Singularity:** A beginning. A point in space-time at which the space-time curvature theoretically becomes infinite. The "singularity theorem" states that a singularity must exist under certain circumstances—particularly that our universe must have begun with a singularity in the Big Bang (pages 61-62).

**Soul:** The unifying principle of life. A construct of pure energy—the synergistic whole that unifies and contains one's spirit, consciousness and thought (pages 51-53).

**Space-time:** The unified expression of the three spatial dimensions and the fourth temporal dimension as postulated in Einstein's Theory of Special Relativity. Einstein established that space and time are really different aspects of the same thing, i.e., space and time rotate into each other—forming the basis of material existence because matter cannot exist without space and time, and vice versa (page 58).

**Special Relativity:** Einstein's revolutionary theory which states that all things in the universe are ultimately measured by their relationship to the speed of light. If a physical object stands at rest or rockets off at an incredibly high velocity, the speed of light, in either instance, remains the same, relative to the object's point of view—that is because time slows down or speeds up in direct proportion to how fast or slow the object is moving. The theory also states that the speed of light is the supreme speed limit in the universe. Nothing else can move as fast as light (because light has no mass). Furthermore, Einstein reasoned that mass and energy are two equivalent aspects of the same thing—the energy expended in an object's movement converts into mass and vice versa (page 42).

**Spirit:** (St. Augustine's definition) "that which is not matter is spirit." The state of existence which transcends the material dimensions of space-time.

**String Theory:** The theory that matter is ultimately made of intricately related modes or frequencies of resonance emanating from tiny vibrating strings (or something that behaves like strings). If we could see the strings, we would find their diminutive size to be that of a Planck length (100 billion billion times smaller than a proton). Moreover, the strings possess the unique properties of being one-dimensional, infinite in length yet infinitely thin, and infinitely curved. The complex dynamics of the strings involve a process in which the strings consistently split, divide, and recombine with each other, conforming with 24 different modes of vibration or resonance (*conformal symmetry*). Furthermore, the strings can be generalized as one vast Superstring. The theory also states that the universe has ten dimensions—because the string, in order to resonate "self-consistently," must vibrate in ten dimensions (pages 59-62). Also, see Ramanujan Modular Function (page 210 g).

**Strong Nuclear Force:** The strongest of the four fundamental natural forces, having the shortest range. It holds atomic and sub-atomic particles together to form atoms.

**Telekinesis:** Also known as psychokinesis. The higher faculty through which one can influence or move a physical object by (telepathically) manipulating its natural resonance (page 13).

**Telepathy:** Transference of thought. The higher faculty through which all spiritual beings transmit or communicate pure, spontaneous, non-verbal thought (page 90).

**Theosophy:** A spiritual philosophy widespread throughout Europe and America during the latter nineteenth century, influenced most prominently by such "mystical esoteric" writers as Madam Helena Blavatsky and Rudolf Steiner. Theosophy teaches a monistic view of the universe as a vast, living organism (not mechanism) in which all living beings are likened to individually evolving entities or cells that comprise a greater universal body. Such a universe is "ever building" in that each individual spirit is an integral, synergistic part of the entire, universal, organic process. One grows and evolves to higher levels of universal consciousness through intuition—this involves exercising and building one's higher faculties, and the pursuit of higher, individual revelation (pages 143, 145).

**Weak Nuclear Force:** The second weakest of the four fundamental, natural forces, with a very short range. It affects all matter particles, but not force-carrying particles.

**Winchester Mystery House:** A monument to higher dimensions and intuitive exercise, the House was built by the late Sarah Winchester, in California's Santa Clara Valley, over a period of thirty-eight years. See Chapter 19 (pages 141-193).

# BIBLIOGRAPHY

Aquinas, St. Thomas. (1947–48). *Summa Theologica*. New York: Benziger Bros.

Brinkley, Dannion. (1994). *Saved By The Light*. With Paul Perry. Villard Books, a division of Random House.

Bryan, William Jennings. (1896). National Democratic Convention.

Eddington, Arthur. (1928). *The Nature of the Physical World*. Cambridge: Cambridge University Press.

Escher, Maurits Cornelis. (1971). *The World of M.C. Escher*. New York: Locher, J.L., Harry N. Abrams, Inc..

Hawking, Stephen. (1988). *A Brief History of Time*. New York: Bantam Books.

Hildegard of Bingen. (1844-91). *Patrologia Latina*, Edited by J.P. Migne, Paris.

Hildegard of Bingen. (1882). *Liber Vitae Meritorum*. Pitra.

Jung, Carl G. (1960). *Psychology and the Occult, The Structure and Dynamics of the Psyche*. Collected works. London: Trevor Hull.

Jung Carl G. (1961). *Memories, Dreams, Reflections*. Recorded and edited by Aniela Jaffe, translated by Richard and Clara Winston. New York: Pantheon Books, a division of Random House, Inc.

Jung, Carl G. (1964). *Man and His Symbols*. Garden City, NY: Doubleday.

Moody, Raymond A. Jr. (1982). Quoted in *A Collection of Near-Death Research Readings,* compiled and edited by Craig L. Lundahl. Chicago: Nelson-Hall Publishers.

Plato. (1942). *The Phaedo*. Translated by B. Jowett, Ed. Louise Ropes Loomis. Roslyn, NY: Walter J. Black.

Radin, Dean (1997). *The Conscious Universe*. San Francisco: HarperEdge.

Swedenborg, Emanuel. (1854). *A Compendium of the Theological and Spiritual Writings of Emanuel Swedenborg*. Boston: Crosby and Nichols, and Otis Clapp.

Webster, A. Merriam. (2000). *Webster's New Collegiate Dictionary*. Springfield, MA: G. & C. Merriam Company.

Widdison, Harold A. (1982). *Near-Death Experiences and the Unscientific Scientist*. Compiled and edited by Craig R. Lundahl, *A Collection of Near-Death Research Readings*. Chicago: Nelson-Hall Publishers.

Williamson, Marianne. (1992). *A Return to Love*. New York: Harper Collins Publishers, Inc.

# INDEX

**Figure 2** *(from page 55)*

*Figure 2 shows four equilateral triangles (forming a tetrahedral pyramid) using the six match sticks. The problem was solved by literally going "up" one higher dimension.*

# About the Author

At the age of nine, Christopher Scott had a "Near-Death Experience." The revelations of that experience have guided him on a life-long odyssey of realization and inquiry into the *ultimate mystery* of existence that is *Beyond Death.* His *Near-Death Experience* also endowed him with a heightened sensibility of such psychic phenomena as mediumship, precognition, and telekinesis.

After several years of intense collegiate studies, Mr. Scott immersed himself on a path of helping people effectively deal with spiritual issues. As a medium and psychic counselor, he has devoted much of his life to serving those in need of spiritual healing, growth, and development. Now, he breaks new ground in the quest for answers to life's most compelling questions: "What really happens when we die? What is the true nature of our universe? Why are we here?" And, "What is the relationship between material and spiritual existence?"

*Beyond Death* is a dizzying, mind-boggling leap into previously uncharted territory in the dimension of the Spirit.

Printed in the United Kingdom
by Lightning Source UK Ltd.
9371300001B